Like a
Watered Garden

Blessings!
Maureen
Is. 58:11

Like a Watered Garden

Maureen Hay Read

Introduction by
Sherwood E. Wirt

HERALD PRESS
Scottdale, Pennsylvania
Kitchener, Ontario

Library of Congress Cataloging in Publication Data

Read, Maureen Hay, 1937-
  Like a watered garden.

  1. Read, Maureen Hay, 1937- 2. Christian
biography—United States. I. Title.
BR1725.R37A34 248'.2'0924 [B] 77-5858

ISBN-13: 978-1601260772
Reprinted in 2008.

Printed 2008 at
Masthof Press
219 Mill Road
Morgantown, PA 19543-9516

To Dad and Mom
in whom abide faith, hope, love,
but the greatest of these is their love.

Contents

Introduction

Maureen Hay came to us "over the transom." That's the expression editors use to describe unsolicited manuscripts. Without querying us in advance, she sent to *Decision* Magazine a story about her visit to the Billy Graham rally at Wembley Stadium, London, in 1966.

The charm with which Maureen wrote, the way she made her point, the obvious love she had for the Lord Jesus Christ, all made their impression upon our staff. Someone else was impressed, too, as these pages reveal. Maureen's is an international story that could only have happened in the world of Billy Graham; and yet she has never met the evangelist. That doesn't matter. She worships the same God and is filled with the same Spirit.

As the wife of Ed Read, Maureen has continued to write and this lovely volume is evidence that she is now a first-rate Christian author. Humor is here, and miracle, and God. Also sadness. The passing of their daughter, Sarah Elizabeth, is handled with chaste feeling and an economy of words that other bereaved parents could well emulate as they write about the loss of their children.

Sometimes in reading personal stories of people, I wonder why they bother to mention God at all; He seems to be dropped in as an afterthought. Not so with Maureen Hay Read. Her faith is so woven into her life that it breathes through every paragraph without ostentation or display.

I know you will enjoy this first book and the warm, human person who wrote it.

Sherwood Eliot Wirt
Editor Emeritus
Decision Magazine

Author's Preface

The Lord shall guide thee
continually,
and satisfy thy soul in drought . . .
and thou shalt be
like a watered garden,
and like a spring of water,
whose waters fail not. —Isaiah 58:11

Over the years I have written down events, thoughts, ideas, meditations, anecdotes, all in a most disorganized way on bits of paper, notebooks, a diary, and even in the margins of my Bible. The time to write my great novel never seemed to be available, however, and in desperation I assembled a few of my notes and sent them off to *Decision* Magazine one day.

No, thanks, not useful to our paper, wrote Dr. Sherwood Wirt, but being my favorite encourager, he told me to develop them into a book. A book? With these? At the time I was busily employed with a colicky first baby and a second already in the manufacturing stage, not to mention a husband and an 86-year-old grandma to care for. There was neither time nor energy to do more than dream.

Gradually though, the babies became preschoolers, the diary and notes accumulated over the years, and I finally gathered them together and began to sort and sift. The exercise gave me perspective and I came to see clearly what I had sensed all along, that God was guiding me all the way, continually He says, and making a watered garden out of unprofitable soil. Fruit—love, joy, peace, patience, faith—these were growing, nourished, and tended by the Master Gardener in spite of weeds of selfishness, the harsh winds of doubt, the burning heat of sorrow.

Jesus, the Water of Life, flowing into me, into you, can make a garden out of a desert.

Maureen Hay Read
Narvon, Pennsylvania

"THE LORD IS MY SHEPHERD, I SHALL NOT WANT."

How could I be so restless, so anxious when I was following Him, the Eternal Shepherd of the sheep? I was, though. Then I realized the strange roundabout path I had been traveling was leading me to the richest experiences of my life.

Follow with me this way and you may remember some of His surprises in your own life.

Prologue

Sitting in the outer reaches of Wembley Stadium one June evening, I first heard that lovely song, "Surely Goodness and Mercy," sung by Beverly Shea and the Crusade Choir. As I sat and watched that huge crowd gather—young people, couples, hippies, white-haired proper English matrons, those who were crippled, tired, cynical, expectant—as I sat observing, my subconscious mind pondered all the years when goodness and mercy had followed me. Often I'd been too preoccupied or thankless to look back. In the perfection of that long English twilight it was fitting to remember and thank God for rich years, full years, brimming with friends, love, kindness, tears, laughter.

Wisps of memory brushed my mind . . . Mom and Dad, what special people they were . . . the secure home we had at Narvon, Pennsylvania, with the beautiful trees and big disorganized house . . . I could hardly wait to get there again . . . the time Jesus became mine as I accepted Him with the sturdy faith of a child . . . Bryan College, many hassles and heartaches then, but also glimpses of higher ground . . . teaching, traveling, trusting. . . .

Bev Shea continued to sing and the words turned into a prayer.

> He restoreth my soul when I'm weary,
> He giveth me strength day by day;
> He leads me beside the still waters,
> He guards me each step of the way.

Oh, Lord, I need some restoration—tonight. I've had three great years in Lebanon, but I'm tired now and a little discouraged.

Like the chaotic traffic of Beirut, people and places rushed down the lanes of my mind. I remembered bouncing across the desert to Baghdad on a bus that broke down endlessly, climbing the steps of the Dhar at Petra and feeling like Moses as he gazed at the Promised Land, sitting in the Garden Tomb on Easter Sunday at dawn. I thought of the thousands of cups of tea I drank with all my friends of the Lebanon Evangelical Mission and the lasting impression they'd made on me, many of them maiden ladies, who had given up everything most women count dearest. I certainly did.

Which brought to mind the hardest struggle of all, one that had been repeated over the years in different circumstances, but grew more difficult as I got older. It had come to a head one evening in Beirut when I paced the flat roof of the junior school and felt the splashes of rain mingle with my tears. It would be an unsuitable and unhappy marriage with Ted, but my heart was deeply involved and refusing was costly. I still felt deep twinges even this night months later. Could one be too particular? Did God require celibacy when every ounce of me longed to love a man totally, to have children, to keep a home?

Father, I'm twenty-eight. I need some reassurance. I trust You, but these doubts and questions keep persisting. Give me some sign that You can still do miracles.

There were miracles all about me that night at Wembley, and I soon forgot my reverie in the excitement of the meeting. I began writing notes on some scraps of paper. Such a huge crowd. How could God ever move it? Billy Graham was just a spot on the platform. No man could reach this vast audience. No man. God did, though, and I was greatly moved by the response.

In the next days I worked the notes into an article, timidly sent it off to *Decision* Magazine, and scampered home to Narvon. After the delight of seeing everyone, I settled in to look for work. Surely God was not going to keep me *here*. Narvon was charming to be sure, but rather less than exotic. Besides there was still this longing to marry Ted, and we were near each other now. God knew better than I what a miserable life we'd both have if we were to marry. Our values, backgrounds, interests were too different. *Surely, Lord, You will help me move somewhere else, far away.*

But He didn't. For some reason I couldn't get out of Narvon that fall, try as I did. Instead I taught in a local high school, very humdrum after Beirut, and endured some bleak, lonely months. When would it end, this ceaseless heart-longing, the strain between love for God and love for man, the daily, hourly cost of decision?

There were some bright spots, of course, times when I forgot. The most spectacular was in November when *De-*

cision published "A Candle at Wembley" and I had the exhilarating experience of seeing myself in print. Then began a flow of fan letters, a crate of oranges from an old flame in Florida, job offers, and my ego was restored. *But Lord, my soul. . . .*

Yes, My dear. Do you remember these words I gave you in Isaiah, "The children which thou shalt have . . . then shalt thou say in thine heart, 'Who hath begotten me these? . . . Behold, I was left alone; these, where had they been?' "

Yes, Lord, I do remember.

Believe them, My dear. I haven't forgotten you.

It was a quiet evening in January when He reminded me of this, after another soul struggle, but this time there was peace and confidence at the end. The battle had finished. And as always, the peace of God is an end in itself. The future was still unknown, Narvon as nonexotic as ever, no prospective dates except with a halfhearted fellow teacher, spring was yet a long way off, but God's priceless peace had enfolded me. *Because the Lord is my Shepherd, I have everything I need.*

o   o   o

When Ed Read's letter came in March, two months later, I knew it was a fan letter by the way it was addressed; it turned out to be the last one I was to receive for that particular article. A Missouri postmark, somewhere off at the end of the world. Clear, decisive handwriting. A sense of space and open country.

The refreshing frankness of the letter startled me into stunned laughter and uncertain admiration. "A bachelor farmer . . . living with an elderly mother . . . admire your spirit, enthusiasm, and humility . . . invite your social

18

correspondence." There was even a small photograph enclosed.

I laughed though I was close to tears. It was the first day of spring, I noted.

Was there a subtle sense of humor in the letter? Maybe he was Irish too? Both the blarney and the name indicated at least a possibility. This was evidently no ordinary farmer whose taste ought to run to the girl down the road with a farm as a dowry. An English teacher and would-be writer was a poor pursuit for a man with acres and equipment and business interests.

Laying the letter aside, I went to New York for the weekend to see my friend, Eleanor. Ambling around the city in the wind and sunshine and hush of Easter Sunday morning, we ended up at the Brick Church. My heart was still sore from the bitterness and heartaches of the winter, but the memory of the first resurrection transcended the pain. And that is one of the glories of the gospel, that it is bigger, wider, deeper, much stronger than these aches of our local life. It contains and comprehends and *conquers* that which seems too great to bear.

Returning to Narvon and Ed Read's letter, I reread it and decided I could now reasonably answer after a week. Lightly, with tongue-in-cheek. After all, he was a farmer and it was spring and he lived in Missouri. Small risk. We'd never meet. Besides, his courage and unusual taste intrigued me. I was fed up at this point with my other interests. This was a welcome diversion.

By return mail his answer came, exuberant because I had written. I winced. He sounded so vulnerable. I was skeptical, having tried this courtship-by-mail before and failing deplorably. Admittedly, I had never corresponded with a man I hadn't even seen, but that made the gamble even greater. It was too much for even my optimism. Apparently his was thriving on it.

Then my little Irish grandmother died and Dad flew over for the funeral. She had possessed all the wisdom and superstition, humor and independence that the Irish are reputed to have and had given me some wonderful grandmotherly memories. With her death Ireland lost some of its charm. I wrote Ed about her and wondered if he had any Irish ancestry. Did he like sports? What kind of farming did he do? And so on.

School was demanding these days. I was involved with junior play practices and hardly noticed until two weeks went by that no letter had come from Missouri. Something must have offended Ed. That was the end of that. God had sent him at a precise time to pull me out of my rut and his mission was accomplished.

Spring was sneaking in despite bleak weather. The lilacs had leaked out and the dogwood were altogether uninhibited in flaunting their pink and white symmetry.

       o   o   o

There was a pile of letters on the table as I came in from school and I settled myself comfortably to savor them all. This was the best part of the day as I visited with friends, all far away, but so near in thought.

And then I noticed that brisk handwriting again. It was a thick letter. Unwilling to speculate, I just read it— and marveled at his persistence. My second letter had never reached him (later he told me his mother had discarded it!) and he was puzzled but pursuing. Did I object to his lack of college? His mother? Farm life? Straightforward, confident, he went into detail about himself, his work, failures, ambition, and closed with the request that if I weren't interested, to let him know immediately.

This man was certainly no one to cast aside lightly. For some reason, he was determined to continue in spite of apparent silence from me unless I gave him a blunt negative response.

That same evening I wrote and the answer was not designed to discourage him.

School ended with a whimper. I was tired and resigned my job. I decided to go to London in late summer, live in an apartment with Rosalind, my friend from Beirut days, and write my best-seller. With money I had saved through the year, I could manage to live economically for some months. A respite from the classroom was probably the chief attraction—that and Rosalind's enthusiasm.

But by now Ed was encouraging me to go to Missouri during the summer months and look the situation over, as he put it. Although the invitation was warm, it didn't suit my inclination. I put out a big test. Could *he* come to Pennsylvania in spite of huge harvests, house-building, intense summer work? His unexpected affirmative reply was just another step along a series of unpredictable, utterly surprising developments in the revelation of this man's character.

One night he phoned. It sent me into a panic with the family and guests eavesdropping at my end. I came through poorly but a series of Sunday night phone calls followed. Was the man mad or could he possibly be the impossible—daring, yet dependable, dominating but tender?

I became suspicious and wondered by mail how many

other girls he had courted by this method? How could such an interesting person be unattached so long? What was wrong with the girls in Missouri? Why hadn't he married before?

The answers were swift, engagingly honest. His character was showing clearly these days. And I could read between the lines as well. A man caring for an inherited farm and aged parents had to be conscientious. And tender. He loved animals and spoke of kittens and calves and piglets. There was a simplicity of faith when he admitted his failure to honor God at one point with an abrupt loss of thousands of dollars as a result. And at the end of one enthusiastic letter, he suggested that "we get down on our knees and thank our heavenly Father," which I did though I hardly knew why.

It is disconcerting to discover oneself in love with an unknown, unseen man. But by mid-July this had happened. For a woman my age, it was a hopelessly irresponsible way to proceed.

The weeks of waiting began to wear. Our friendship had suddenly and unreasonably and incredibly become deadly serious. I scoffed at myself. Waves of fear, self-ridicule, inexplicable hope, and panic surged through me. A wet wheat season delayed his visit a few weeks longer than we had planned and I was tempted to throw the whole thing over and take off for London where my Beirut friends had migrated during the Six-Day War.

And then Ed himself seemed to be attacked for the first time with doubts. For sweet pity's sake, let's not get cold feet now. I wanted at least to meet and be disillusioned properly. My plans were to go immediately to London should the dream burst. By now nearly a week had passed without a letter from him and I was sure he was backing out in spite of a warm phone call.

Letters never came in the evening mail, but Mom persuaded me to check at the post office anyway. And my heart which had mourned privately all afternoon while I cleaned the guest room, glowed as I saw the familiar writing.

He was coming. In fact he was even then leaving the Joplin railroad station as I read the letter, scheduled to arrive in Lancaster thirty-six hours later. He would sleep at a hotel awhile, clean up, and phone when he felt up to facing the Hay clan.

Peace came, smothering forever all the fears and tears of the day and the summer. There was a natural excitement, but the fretting had gone. Whether lovable or not, he had kept his word every time. He would be there on Sunday, for better or for worse.

° ° °

How does one meet a man who has declared his love, exposed his character, shared his dreams, all sight unseen? It somehow reminded me of our friendship with Christ, whom having not seen we love, as Peter so aptly put it.

The phone call came on Sunday as promised.

Driving the twenty miles to Lancaster, I sang songs, thought long thoughts, anything to divert myself. I still could not believe a man could sound so good and be free so long. At the beginning of summer, I should have obeyed his invitation, sneaked out to Missouri, and nipped it in the bud. Too late now.

Such a lot of traffic today. I wonder what we'll say to each other. And I'm not half so good-looking as he ex-

23

pects. That's so important to a man. It's taking forever to get there. Oh, help, I don't even know where that hotel is.

Getting directions from a service station, I finally parked in front of the hotel and pranced in. It was somehow oddly all right to go in and pick up a perfect stranger. There were two men in the lobby. One was obviously not Ed, the other was buried behind a newspaper which was typical, I later found out. Peering around the paper, I said hi.

Blue eyes with friendly crinkles at the edges, a firm mouth, keenly sensitive and alert, an easy laugh. We stood and talked, sat and looked, grinned widely, collected our wits, and walked out. I often wondered if the desk clerk ever noticed this small drama.

As I drove through the traffic rather madly, Ed made a mild comment about it and chuckled when I said it was his fault. We sang, we talked, we laughed, we were silent, we loved.

To the Liberty Bell for a brief look and home again from all the traffic that Ed hated. Rambling around the fabled farms of Lancaster County. Visiting and driving. Covertly and overtly watching each other. For three days.

The clan was impressed, for the first time in the history of my boyfriends. Not that that was necessary. It was simply a pleasant and remarkable fringe benefit.

I had always scoffed privately at people who said the right person paled all previous loves. That sounded too romantically idealistic. But cynic or not, that's exactly what happened to me. It was there and it would be there as long as there was an Ed and a Maureen. The ecstasies and heartbreaks of my past faded. They were all a part of me, and I couldn't and wouldn't deny them for anything. I was a richer person for them, but they no longer intruded upon my life.

What attracted me to him? The quality that had originally caught my attention was his courage and strange taste. Then his loyalty to family, farm, and friends bespoke dependability. Yet his ambitious, occasionally wild agricultural schemes disclosed a streak of daring. As time went on, I discovered the dreary loneliness and hard work that had been his lot for many years. Though he never once complained, it was written on his face. I sensed that the easy laugh was sometimes a camouflage for scars.

All of this I did not learn right away, for Ed does not reveal himself easily. I did learn, though, that life with this man would be different from all I ever expected. And the unexpected and unusual were never unattractive to me.

All the years of wandering and working were amply compensated. God who had seemed to loiter for such a long time was in reality deliberately and diversely preparing two people to be one. The niche that had eluded me was here in the heart and arms of this man from Missouri, one of the last places I would have searched.

The echo came from a drab Paris hotel room years before. "He that goeth forth and weepeth, bearing precious seed, shall doubtless come again with rejoicing." I had read that verse one lonely night on the way to Beirut—and wondered if it were *really* true. It was. Suppose I had never gone to teach in Beirut nor stopped in England to hear Billy Graham at Wembley Stadium on the way home; suppose I had never written my impressions of that great meeting and submitted them to *Decision;* suppose Ed had never reacted to the article and I had not responded to him. Suppose.

Only God would use such a circuitous route. In His own fullness of time.

◦　◦　◦

Ed returned to Missouri and asked me to follow by air. I did a few days later, on my birthday. He had let the news out and when I got there, apparently half of Jasper County were agog over Ed Read's latest adventure. I received a warm welcome even from his very black, very ancient tomcat who certainly needed some feminine attention.

Ed was building a new house where I stayed the next weeks while he and his mother lived in the tiny old house. She was 85, as she proudly told me, and quite dubious about a newcomer, but decided that a cook was a useful thing to have around. As time went on, we became fond of each other in spite of ourselves.

Such open, spacious country. For a while I missed the hills of my native Pennsylvania, but then discovered the sky instead. It was so enormous with nothing to hide it. Sunsets, multi-starred nights, clouds pacing one another, trees leaning in the wind.

Ed worked hard on his farms and I was busy sanding and varnishing the woodwork in the new house. It was tedious and tiring but poring over each room and cupboard and window, I learned to appreciate Ed's planning, the size and beauty of the home. Helping complete it made it mine in a special way.

The woodwork finally finished, we began carpet shopping. We chose strong colors—gold, bright red, moss-green, blue. The rich rarity of our romance demanded brilliance, no muted shades at all.

I had always imagined that if and when I married, I would find myself in some stark missionary quarters in a South American jungle or a drab parsonage near a village church. To choose new furniture, scrub shining bathroom fixtures, and play with a garbage disposal were pleasures I hadn't counted on. It was the exceedingly abundant above all I asked or even thought which I should have learned to expect from a God of hyperbole.

One morning I drove to Carthage, paced the pavement a few minutes until Ramsay's opened, and then walked in and chose material for a wedding dress. White satin with some exquisite lace for trim. I wished for Rosalind or someone to share the subdued delight. Walking around the square to the car, I felt joy seeping out of me like the color from the sugar maples. All the years of waiting with the muddles and bitterness and heartaches and fun and falls had been worthwhile.

The wind tussled with my hair, the sky was blue, a feel of autumn in the air. I drove to the farm and made shepherd's pie for dinner, from the sublime to the mundane.

"HE MAKETH ME TO LIE DOWN IN GREEN PASTURES."

The first year of married life in our new home in the middle of the farm was just this: resting in green pastures. God had taken me out of a very active life and put me out to pasture. Now I had time to play with the dog and pamper some roses, time to drink coffee with a neighbor and can applesauce. And best of all, time to dream of and pray for that little life inside of me.

Sit with me awhile in these pleasant pastures, smile with me over some of the problems, and remember your own times of renewal with Him.

CHAPTER 1

LITTLE STRANGER

December 5, 1967

December second was my wedding day.

I stood alone at the top of the stairs, except for little Melissa and her three-year-old chatter. Yet how could I possibly be alone when accompanied by hosts of friendships past and present, memories sad and joyous tumbling over themselves for recognition, a thousand places and people piercing into my mind? I felt akin to Infinity, able to open my arms and grasp all that so enriched me and brought me to that moment. My life, intense and crowded, had yielded abundantly and I tried to savor every bit in those few moments of waiting.

There was a medley of emotion. "The bride eyes not her garment, but her dear Bridegroom's face/ I will not gaze at glory, but on my King of grace." Peg was singing the words that reminded me poignantly of one who was now with her heavenly Bridegroom. It had been sung at Alice McLeod's wedding and two years later at her funeral.

31

"Grampie is at the bottom of the stairs," Melissa whispered loudly. "I want to go down."

Grampie was indeed there coughing and gulping as he waited to give his firstborn away. This day was one that he in his wisdom had prayed for, but it was also one that hurt his tender Irish heart, a heart uncannily attuned to my own.

The perfume of my red roses . . . down the creaking stairs to the lovely formality of the wedding march . . . Melissa in her wee red dress bearing my train . . . Ed's eyes shining . . . his chuckle of delight as he spied Melissa with the drooping train . . . Dearly beloved, we are assembled here in the presence of God, to join this man and this woman in holy marriage . . . I, Maureen, take thee, Edward, to be my wedded husband . . . Our Father, which art in heaven, hallowed be Thy name . . . that great encompassing prayer joining a fellowship of friends who bathed me in love, friends in Beirut, London, Ireland, Vietnam, Narvon . . . love in that room pouring over me from my family . . . Ed's love, the lonely discipline of years at last able to give of all its fullness to me . . . The Lord bless thee and keep thee and make His face to shine upon thee . . . the kiss of my husband.

Then began the post-wedding confusion of food, photographs, congratulations, gifts, perpetual smiles till my face hurt. Alice Fredricks, recently married, rejoiced with me over the gracious leading of God in our lives. There was the quiet, totally unselfish joy of Aunt Sadie and Aunt Ruth who never had a wedding day of their own. The Martins whom I had mothered off and on so many years beamed at us even though they've grown big and apart now. Mom wetly smiled—then we were off.

The beauty and excitement drained away leaving impressions that were ours to carry through the years ahead. Perhaps the loveliest of all was the memory of my husband reading Proverbs 31 to me that same evening. "Who can find a virtuous woman? for her price is far above rubies. The heart of her husband doth safely trust in her. . . . She will do him good." No matter what are the losses and gains, sorrows and joys, pains and pleasures of our future, it is all arranged by God. Nothing can shake that assurance from my mind, and beside that fact, all else is insignificant. The love of my husband enveloped me and the love of our God covered and held us both.

December 8, 1967

I'm feeling such joy sitting in our shining kitchen with sunshine outside, music inside, and love all around, tangibly demonstrated by gifts from many near and far. What fun I've had caressing towels, playing with the electric can opener, trying to match colors and rooms. I am savoring it all.

Today I've been thinking of those I love who are lonely, who can't share in my happiness. Lord, don't let me grow thoughtless and indifferent.

January 20, 1968

I've got me a desk, a little, old-fashioned one that belonged to Ed's grandfather. Here I can read and write and watch the sunsets and think long thoughts. Every nook of this house is becoming so special and so mine.

The snow has melted, the earth is black and moist, the birds and I are getting spring fever.

Ed and I have had some talks about finances, personal problems, our love. That miracle never ceases to amaze me. He had to give up one of his farms, a hard, humiliating loss. He's tossing around some ideas for the future.

My mind is cudgeling some thought to write—a book perhaps? It sounds presumptuous.

I'm longing for a baby.

May 6, 1968

The small events of life are what in the long run make up our attitudes and general bent, much more than the great happenings. Things like cooking a satisfactory meal, watching flowers grow, feeding our big boisterous dog, getting a letter. We learn habits of emotion and mind that make up the tone of our life, and these are preparation for the crises and big decisions that inevitably come.

We are busier now that spring is here. Ed has been custom plowing. One day Mrs. Read and I took him lunch and we had a picnic by the side of the field. I love to do such errands, but wish I could go unaccompanied. It is hard to know how much privacy I should expect and demand.

Am I pregnant?

May 30, 1968

I *am* pregnant. The doctor confirmed it on Tuesday and still I can hardly believe it. Driving home from his office, I felt like spring, life bursting in the ground, the trees, inside of me. Right now a soft rain is falling and shining mistily in the sun. There is the most lovely rainbow outside, a reminder again that God's promises are never broken. I remember once more His promise to me two years ago, "The children which thou shalt have. . . . Who hath begotten me these?"

Feeling nausea and weariness. The price of motherhood is sometimes high, I suppose, but the loneliness of barrenness is higher.

June 24, 1968

After heavy heat a beautiful rain is soaking the earth. I just returned from a walk to Wynona's and loved the cold splashes on my face.

Our little one is doing what he's supposed to, I guess. My baby. It's still hard to realize. Nothing concerns me except the child be well and strong.

Bobby Kennedy and Martin Luther King are dead so tragically. Disillusionment with the war and with our own government. Credibility gaps. Some I love are turning into cynics. I must somehow convey faith and hope through something I write.

August 1, 1968

Was there ever mother-in-law like mine? I smile even now as I overhear her mumbling outside, "Where's that swat? Doggone fly?" And trudging up the steps into the house, "Maroon, I can't find that fly. Where's Ed? Don't you know where Ed is? He oughtta be home before dark." And outside again, constantly restless, looking for spiders or flies. Poor hapless creatures, her aim is remarkably accurate for one 86 years old. She gets a grisly pleasure in using the old scissors to cut enormous green tomato worms in two, which is okay with me. I can't stand the creatures.

"Guess I'll water some flowers. Where's the bucket? Oh, I'm too tired. I'll get some milk. Maroon, what are we going to have for supper? We ought to have something for supper." It is 3:00 p.m. I suggest a snack but she wants "something hot" to eat. Eventually she gives up and eats two bowls of cereal and some bread. An incredible appetite apparently is the secret of her health and energy.

My special pet peeve is to be awakened in the morning with her walking into the bedroom, telling me to get up and make some breakfast. Mornings are not my specialty anyway.

I always feel guilty sneaking away to town for various errands, but it's almost impossible to get away without her if she knows. And to quarrel with her just wears me out. So off I go during one of her very brief rests which I sometimes miscalculate and then she discovers me. The break is good for both of us, necessary for me. When I drive in, she is holding the door open, as excited as a child at what I buy. "Here's some sugar. What are you going to make with the sugar? A cake would be good. I'm hungry. Make me some supper. Where's Ed? He has no business over there. Who did you see in town? I played the piano while you were gone. And picked zinnias." There would be our sixth bouquet.

At night she always checks to know where the keys to the Ford are. Looking here and there, asking a dozen times, she locates them at last, and then goes off to bed. Perhaps to stay, more likely to come back and turn off lights, check the front door—or to eat.

She's difficult to live with, there's no doubt about it, but I'm hoping we can manage. For Ed's sake especially.

36

August 14, 1968

While still in bed yesterday, I felt the first flutter of life, a tiny involuntary kick. Ed was with me and I was thrilled to feel it then and share the excited joy. He calls it the little stranger.

The three great loves of my life—Jesus, whom having not seen I love, Ed, who won my heart even before I met him, and now this little one inside me who grows dearer every day. I am longing to hold him. I loved all of them *before* I saw them, the miracle of faith and hope and love all intertwined.

August 22, 1968

Happiness is . . .

Sitting on the front porch with morning breezes blowing, sewing my new maternity dress . . .

Roses blooming . . .

Husband walking in from the shed and his smile . . .

A birthday dinner where Ed took me just one year ago. He is dearer than ever tonight . . .

My little one moving inside, no doubt enjoying the dinner too . . .

The goodness of God . . .

November 24, 1968

I walked down the south field feeling as gay as my red scarf and gloves. The day was not really cold, the wind soft and making a friendly rustling sound through the dried milo stalks. Feeling heavy with child, I enjoyed the dog who stampeded down the lane behind me and past before he stopped, whirled, and returned again.

My wee one occasionally wiggled within. I thought of

Mary and mothers of all ages, every one thrilling to the hope, all the same, yet each time so totally new, each woman alone in her contemplation of agony and exceeding joy.

The pain seemed unimportant now as I gamboled clumsily with the dog. Before too many years I would be walking down this field with my child, perhaps my children.

A dark thought. The uncertainties of life. Suppose, suppose, like many others, I never saw my child grow up. I know Ed would love and cherish this small one. And so would God. So often He mentions orphans—no need to doubt there. Love is the thing. No one is ever deprived so long as he is loved.

November 28, 1968

Lord, thank you for the bleakness of November and the glory of chrysanthemums. Yellow, copper, white. For the warmth of my home, the deep-green richness of the drapes, the comfort of the red rocker, the big white family Bible.

My kitchen. The friendly warmth of an old-fashioned kitchen and the convenience of a modern one. The maple chairs and table, wide window framing sunrises and moonrises, green canisters and oatmeal cookies, and stainless steel pots and windowed ovens at eye-level.

Stereo playing Christmas carols. Your birth, Lord, and the hope and cheer that has seeped through the ages because of that silent night.

Memories. Friends, places, children, love. How rich I am. Neighbors and cups of coffee.

Friendly dog and old black tomcat.

My husband. A depth of love and loyalty that stumbles in expression but is dependable and durable. That he needs me and I need him, the grace of giving.

The movement of life. Our little stranger, greatly loved though still unseen. Lord, to think You once lived within a woman.

O come, let us adore Him. Amen.

December 5, 1968

Long, long thoughts of Mary and her expectation that first Christmas as she awaited her little morsel of God-man. To think that God entrusted Himself to mortal flesh, that He who inhabited eternity filled one small womb, that He submitted to the protection and hovering care of a mother.

I marvel at the condescension of God. And in His humility, I see His greatness increased, and I learn again that in loss and limitation there is great gain.

December 21, 1968

Such a feeling of lighthearted joy and bodily heaviness these days. Sitting in church I had tender thoughts of our little stranger and sober ones of Mary's Little Stranger. "He was in the world, and the world was made by him, and the world knew him not." Always a Stranger. Such aching loneliness and active hatred pursued Him through life, yet because of that dreary hardship and pain, my little one is given love and welcome and hope. "The people that walked in darkness have seen a great light . . . which lighteth *every man* that cometh into the world."

That light is still shining.

December 26, 1968

No baby for Christmas and it wasn't for lack of concentration. However, in its own good time. "When the fullness of the time was come. . . ."

The astronauts are coming back from their ten moon orbits and the whole world is still agog at the wonder of it. They read from Genesis chapter 1 on Christmas Eve, a moving thing.

I cried all day, or so it seemed, on Christmas Eve. Homesickness, no baby, and Mrs. Read was extremely difficult. Finally Ed, the peacemaker, came home. He and I sat by our baby tree and thought and reminisced and talked. It was a beautiful evening.

He is interested in a printing franchise which sounds good, but I have big reservations. I can't imagine him tied down to a confining business. He needs the freedom of the farm. Once we give it up, we can't return.

Mom phoned last night. She sounded lonely.

January 16, 1969

On the twelfth day of Christmas, January 6, our son was born. So fair from the beginning, big blue eyes that rolled wonderingly, wee fingers perfect to the smallest fingernail. I held out my arm and the nurse laid him beside me while Ed stood by the bed and we were a *family*.

There had been mindless agony, more than I dreamed possible. Then in the dawn my little mite was born— new, naked, and weeping with heartbreaking innocence.

Such pain and humiliation in childbirth and then infinite dignity. I have given birth to a baby, a man-child, a living soul.

Ed was waiting outside the delivery room. "Did you see him? I guess he wasn't very pretty then." And I loved his spontaneous reply, "Oh, but he's a *dear* baby."

A dear baby.

February 13, 1969

These have been hard weeks with little rest. Neighbors like Wynona and Violet Lewis have helped as much as they can, but I seem to be worn out. James has had severe colic.

How can I complain? I feed him and inspect those fat cheeks. Even His knees are getting dimples now. The exuberant health of well-fed babyhood in a setting of morning sunshine and comfortable kitchen and old-fashioned rocker.

Oh, Lord, remember those who lack so much. I thought of Biafra and the bony-legged, large-bellied starving children there. There would be babies weeping pitifully and young children who know nothing but gnawing stomach and craving eyes. Small ones everywhere hungry for food, love, understanding, homes. Jesus said, "Suffer the little ones to come unto me. . . . ." An invitation they've never heard, or they would surely come to One so kind.

My little James, you have so much—love, food, and warmth—and one day soon you will know Him, the Lover of small children, and maybe you will share Him with those in need.

February 20, 1969

He cries so often. In the weariness of night I hear his wail, sometimes hours apart, more often just minutes.

What could he possibly need now? I've fed, burped, changed, cuddled him, and he's still not satisfied. More milk? A stuck burp? Maybe he sensed my tired impatience and needs assurance. Or he'd like to be turned over. Colic? Not in the middle of the night, I hope. I simply can't get out of bed again.

But I do. "Can a woman forget her sucking child?"

Interpreting a baby's cry—how often God has to interpret my cry. "We know not what we should pray for as we ought: but the Spirit itself maketh intercession for us." A mother uses her judgment and guesses what her child needs. God hears our panicked, plaintive cries (Help me! God bless us all. Keep me from danger.) and in His wisdom He interprets the yell and sends what we need. It may not be what we ask for; in our fretful impatience we demand lavishly, but God who looks out for sparrows and lilies is well able to sense our spoken and unspoken needs and supply them richly.

March 21, 1969

Today Ed stopped being a farmer. He had a public sale and sold most of his machinery and odds and ends around the place. Two of his farms have already been sold. I am disappointed but know he has had a bad year and has been thoroughly discouraged. He is buying an instant printing franchise to set up in Springfield, but we plan to live here on the farm and rent the land. I'm praying it will work out.

April 6, 1969 (Easter)

Over the years I've had such memorable Easters. Jerusalem and the sunrise service at the Garden Tomb,

Baghdad after a mad trip across the desert on a bus, the quiet Sunday morning streets of New York City, and the dignity of the Brick Church when I grasped the greatness of the gospel and the meanness of my own local aches and complaints—and that was the same week Ed wrote me for the first time.

This year I'm Ed's wife and James' mother. No particular drama or excitement fill our little country church but the peace of forgiveness, the hope of eternal life, and the love of a family are precious to me.

"I am come that they might have life, and that they might have it more abundantly."

Thank you, Lord, for the abundance.

"HE LEADETH ME BESIDE THE STILLED WATERS."

The turbulent waters of the hills of Judea had to be stilled for the sheep to drink. The shepherd would make a quiet pool out of the boiling, tumbling creeks and lead the sheep to them. My waters were beginning to run faster, stirred with strife and fear. Only Jesus, the Shepherd, could calm them into pools of clarity and refreshment, and lead me to them.

Share the stilled waters here and there as the pace of my life increased and burdens grew heavier.

CHAPTER 2

MEAT LOAF OR CHILI?

May 18, 1969

This is incredible. Evidently our precautions were ineffective. For several weeks there has been a familiar queasiness, constant tiredness, so that I know there must be another little one on the way. At least I needn't worry about having an only child. And at our age why should we wait?

I've been rather green teaching Bible school each day, and Ed has been in California learning how to run his franchise. It seems lonely here. James is just now getting over his colic. Between these two babies I feel a little shopworn. Grandma hasn't helped matters either. She follows me and constantly worries about meals, the baby, how I should fry the bacon, where Ed is, until I finally snap at her and then repent the rest of the day. I would give a whole lot to have just one meal by ourselves, to hang up clothes without her following me and turning the socks around, to take James for a walk and not be told it's too cold or too hot.

Yet she is pitiable and lonely. I know this, but still feel so resentful at times. I pray for patience and in one instant it's gone.

It looks like a long haul this summer with Ed in Springfield so late each day.

July 28, 1969

James has sobbed himself to sleep and his mother has sat here and cried with him. It's so hard to listen to him, easier to give in and cajole and spoil. But it seems right to make him learn to sleep without so much attention.

I wonder if God weeps with us when we cry for what we want. How easy it would be for Him to give in to us and yet He doesn't. He supplies our *needs*, not our wants.

August 4, 1969

My little boy surrounded by toys: a shiny teapot, his favorite; a shampoo bottle; plastic lids and plates. Talking busily to each in turn, an interested eye on old black tomcat, feet kicking incessantly. Two or three Cheerios cling to his damp diaper, all the better for eating to be nice and soggy. Such blithe indifference to sanitation.

How good of God to give Ed and me such a dear little boy.

August 19, 1969

A flurry of company lately, all in rapid succession, but I enjoyed it immensely. I've been hungry for people. Ed is in Springfield long days and it's been *hot*. I'm never at my best then.

The business is slow and he's a little discouraged. I

wish that I could be involved, that we were nearer and I could drop in on the business each day to cheer him and let him go out to drum up trade, that I could window-shop and show off my little boy, that I could have a break from Grandma.

I can't. Lord, help me to be content.

November 8, 1969

There was the most un-November-like weather all week, clear and balmy. How James and I enjoyed it.

I've been on a window-washing spree and this afternoon Ed washed the outside ones for me. He didn't want me climbing; I'm so clumsy now. It's good to be loved and looked after. James and I watched our daddy from vantage points inside and listened to Christmas carols on the stereo. Happiness indeed.

November 17, 1969

What a pathetic sight is a little sick boy. James got severe diarrhea and couldn't shake it for several days till he had an effective medicine. He would try to crawl after me and end up in a little tired heap, unable to move. I've thought a lot about children who have no medicine or care or food. What utter heartbreak to watch your child in need and not be able to help at all.

January 2, 1970

Our first Christmas with James and he was good-humored, happy, delightful to watch. We had a little fat tree which he touched curiously, ouched, then steered clear of.

The other day we had snow but I encouraged Ed to

drive home from Springfield anyway. (I don't like nights without him.) He flipped the car into the ditch and damaged it a little, himself not at all. But the thought of him hurt or dead—because of me—was unbearable. I love him.

He's discouraged these days with the business. What would we do without prayer?

January 29, 1970

Our little Sarah Elizabeth hurried into the world last Sunday morning, January 25, after just a couple hours work on my part. The water broke at 5:00 a.m. and the contractions were less than five minutes apart from the start. Ed and I deliberated over a boy's name between pains since he didn't like the one he had chosen. (For a girl we had already decided to remember both grandmas.) I got ready and he was still tidily shaving. By the time we left the house, pushed out by Mom, I *knew* the time was near.

After weeks of snowy weather, she was born on a brilliant warm morning as the light of dawn was coming through the windows. It was a special delight to hear the nurse say, "A girl." Ever since I was small, I planned on a girl.

She was born with her mind made up. I'm trying to get her convinced to stay awake by day and asleep by night, but it's no use. I'm worn out with her schedule. She doesn't settle down until 2:00 a.m. or *after* and James and Grandma come on strong by 6:30 at the latest. Yet I've thought so much of Mrs. Arnold at the hospital when I was there. She lost her little girl and would give a lot to sit up at night as I'm doing.

Ed is prospering a little more, but not enough really to be worthwhile. I'm praying.

February 24, 1970

The loveliest times of the day are those when I sit in the red rocker feeding Elizabeth and watching James play. Her face intent, wee hands pushed into fists against her face, a curl on the top of her head—and I keep trying to impress it all into my motherly memories. James is mastering his blocks, looking at books, and pointing at the pictures with a fat forefinger and little chirps that are his language.

Sunday he walked for Ed and both of them were thrilled.

The business is still a concern and Ed is talking about selling it. For his sake I am sorry.

March 16, 1970

A snowstorm today, the second in less than a week, is unthinkable. It's beautiful, clinging white stuff but I'm in no mood to enjoy it at this time of year. Ed will no doubt stay in Springfield again and the night is dreary without him—especially when Elizabeth cries a long time.

Such a limited mind I've got these days. I must fold the diapers . . . where's the pacifier . . . when did Elizabeth last eat . . . James, don't untie your shoes . . . meat loaf or chili for supper? Where, oh where, are my great ideas, my book manuscript? There's not even time for the *Reader's Digest*. I can't think coherently for half a minute. Two babies and an 88-year-old grandma do not stretch one's mind nor expand one's horizon appreciably.

The echo of one who lived in a small, narrow world but who reaches to the limits of time and history, "Inasmuch as ye have done it unto one of the least of these. . . ."

April 24, 1970

Is there a sweeter sound than the patter of little feet in the morning? I lay in bed today while Ed got James up and in half wakefulness I heard him running up and down the hall with his teddy bear.

Elizabeth is a darling. She laughs out loud and gets prettier every day.

June 3, 1970

Life is such a wispy thing. We grasp it, cherish it, and in a breath it is gone. I was reminded of my own mortality again recently by a persistent hoarseness which my fertile imagination diagnosed as cancer of the throat. It turned out to be overtiredness compounded by my usual drainage problem, an annoying but not serious ailment.

Then Dad fell at work and broke both arms and injured his back quite severely. My indestructible father nearly as helpless as our baby girl. They all came to see us, Uncle Thomas and Aunt Katy over for a few weeks from Ireland, Mom, Dad all bandaged, and it was a picture to see Elizabeth sitting on his lap with his big casts and a brace on his back. I never saw Dad so thin nor unshaven before.

The business is sold now and Ed is groping for his niche. Several possibilities haven't jelled as he had hoped. His nerves have been bad. I've been tired. The babies and Grandma seem to keep me a little frazzled.

Yet I have them. A dear little boy and girl. And I'm not pregnant yet!

July 1, 1970

The foolishness of a mother. I fondly thought I had both babies asleep and sat peacefully reading a book till suddenly overcome with weariness. To bed happily.

James was crying. I lurched out of bed muttering to Ed who answered automatically and kept on sleeping. Wet pants, a long drink, the fan on full blast. Mercy, it's a hot night.

I'm drugged again and I hear James crying again. More wet pants, *how* do little boys manage it so often, another drink, five raisins, oh-nice-teddy-to-sleep-with-and-here's-your-little-book-now-James-go-to-sleep-like-a-good-boy-blah-blah.

No use going back to bed. Elizabeth is stirring. Chewing her fists, her blanket, starved to death just three hours after her last bottle. Change her pants. She'll need cereal so I can guarantee her sleeping till morning. Ha, babies come with no guarantees whatever. She's thrilled with the light on the stove and I can hardly see straight. We spill some. Grab the dishcloth. Glub, slurp, ptpt, good cereal. Now a bottle.

Mmmm. Wonder if the fans are too strong. We don't need summer colds. I'll turn James' off him. Too strong.

Back in bed, I hear him again. Too hot? He is. The same routine again, minus the wet pants. *Now* James, go to sleep. Firmly. He understands. But as I drop off again, I hear him chirping to himself. Oh no, is he waking again? That fan . . .?

But we all sleep a couple hours and then I remember

53

the fans again. At least I have sense not to turn them off. The noise invariably wakens them at that time of night. I'll just turn them away from a direct breeze. Is that Ed stirring? He prowls around awhile, the bathroom, refrigerator, brush-teeth circuit and then we're settled again.

Just a usual bumpy summer night. At least no thunderstorms. Be thankful for small blessings.

July 12, 1970

I cheerfully planted nasturtiums in two long elegant green boxes and set them on the porch. The moles could not touch them and the dog was too busy digging for moles to bother.

He wasn't. The first day he had dug a big hole in the end of each one. A few days later tomcat decided the width was just his size and he perched there on top of some fragile little plants. Then James discovered the "lowrs." He pinched them off and showed me the tender green leaves and stalks.

Still they grew. How lovely to have brilliant orange nasturtiums falling over the sides of the porch. One morning I got up and they were gone, clean gone. Some wretched fat worms had feasted all the night and there was nothing but a few green stalks left.

James used the dirt to make nice squishy mud pies.

August 15, 1970

The infinity of minutiae with babies. Diapers, the pail is always full especially after I was up seven times last night with one or both.

Puddles to wipe up. Shoes to polish for church and the

laces to wash and hang up where I'll remember to find them. Little clothes to fold. Toys to pick up endlessly. Sorting out pots and lids and cans garnered from cupboards and scattered afield.

A vast effort in logistics at bedtime. I bathe them together in the double kitchen sink and have to have everything on hand. Once they're in, I must take care that they don't topple out. They're a picture to see and have grand fun together. So do I watching them. They are worth every tired bone and sleepless night.

August 22, 1970

I am now 33 years old, the age of Christ when He died. It *is* an age of "perfect" maturity. Only One who had lived completely could understand all of the weariness, grief, loneliness, and sin of man. Had He died at 20, the death would not have sufficed in the same way. And had He lived to be fifty or sixty, there would not have been the same tragedy in His death.

Tragedy, yet triumph.

"THY ROD AND THY STAFF THEY COMFORT ME"

The wolves of weariness and want, the mists of discouragement and fear surrounded me. But Jesus' rod was bigger than the wolves of bitterness and exhaustion and He could conquer them—when I let Him. And His staff, how comforting to know that with it He kept me by His side in spite of doubt and fear, even when I tried to run.

Share with me these confused tired days and find His comfort as I did.

CHAPTER 3

THREADS AND KNOTS

September 1, 1970

What are we doing wrong? I'm pregnant again. Yesterday I started feeling sick and was sure of it then. At least this one will be a spring baby. No need to worry about getting to the hospital in a January snowstorm. I'm even very happy. I wanted three children at least, and in the long run it's best if they're close.

But the short run is hard. There's a weary eighteen months ahead: pregnancy, and then all the early infancy colic, diapers, and sleeplessness. Maybe this one will go to bed on time.

And maybe Ed will find something that's both satisfying and profitable to do. So far there have been constant frustrations for him.

November 5, 1970

Traveling is never easy. I know that. To travel alone with two-and-a-third babies is pushing the point a little. To go during an air strike is asking for punishment.

59

Loaded down with various equipment, Ed drove us the 150 miles to Kansas City to insure a through flight to Philadelphia. Instead we found it was rerouted and we'd have a layover in Chicago. I met up with another mother and baby-in-arms who helplessly attached herself to me. We sat together on the plane, two mothers and three squirming babies with one inside me compounding the airborne feeling. At least all the spitting up and messy pants were in a small space, much to the hostess's relief. Cutting a steak while holding Elizabeth up out of reach (she wiggled nonstop), overseeing James' supper beside me, and dispensing help to my seatmate and child all made the trip go fast at least.

It was a terrific effort, the return trip even worse, but I was so hungry to see everyone back East again. I've got to share these little ones with all my family and friends. They grow so fast.

But I'm bone-tired as a result.

December 1, 1970

How fragile a thing is marriage, yet how durable. A look, a word amiss, an unexplained silence can puncture it. Yet the simplest thing—a kiss, a meeting of eyes, a word fitly spoken will mend it again.

Tomorrow is our third anniversary. I have so much—a good husband, a lovely home, two darling children. Yet I've been gripy lately. Our financial concerns seem to have got on top of me, and I'm tense, emotional, critical. Nothing has worked out for Ed; he keeps hitting dead ends.

I have left off constant prayer and it has become a hurried thing. *That* is the real fault, I suppose.

January 7, 1971

An ordinary day. James wanted to go to "Aunt Nonie's" and I did too for that matter. It's a major operation though in the wintertime.

1. Warm up the pickup.
2. Take James to the bathroom.
3. Put on his coat and hat.
4. Explain to Grandma that we're going to Wynona's.
5. Change Elizabeth's pants.
6. Put on her coat and hat which she loathes. Tie *securely*.
7. Explain to Grandma that we're going . . . etc.
8. Put on my coat and hat.
9. Explain to Grandma . . . etc.
10. Carry James out to the pickup and push in the choke. It stalls. Start it again.
11. Explain . . . etc.
12. Carry Elizabeth out after checking her pants again.
13. Tell Grandma please to keep the door closed and look out the window.
14. Push in the choke and it stalls again. Start motor and keep choke out this time.
15. Hope Wynona is home and will make a pot of coffee.

She was and she did. Bless her.

March 20, 1971

It was a perfectly wild Saturday morning. Grandma needed a bath very much. I told Ed, who told her, and there was a big hassle over that. Finally the mission was accomplished with great rumblings, complaints, commands.

I scurried around to find clean and dirty clothes, clean ones so she wouldn't put the dirty ones on again and I could quickly wash them.

Ed was to cut her toenails. More grumbles. It was quite a project but he never loses patience with her. It looked quite menacing. He ended up using clippers, a razor blade, and a knife. I suggested soaking her feet awhile, but that was too easy.

All was progressing nicely. Our ancient wash machine was going into its spin cycle which sounded like a tornado approaching, I had Grandma's shoes up high so Elizabeth wouldn't eat them, my hair was washed, the babies dressed, the dishes soaking. For the moment everything was under control.

Then Grandma lost her glasses which always panicked her. Ed and she searched everywhere or at least walked around in circles. They even checked the washer and dryer.

I decided to look. The suspense was too much. They were on her bed.

By 9:30 a.m. Grandma was starved. I was still doing breakfast dishes.

I put the dishcloths in the utility sink to soak in bleach. Grandma cleared her throat and uh-oh, I think it landed in the sink. It did.

Make beds, roll hair, read to kids, put meat in oven to thaw (I had forgotten to take it out) wash more clothes, take an aspirin.

It wasn't my morning. James spilled a whole loaf of bread on the floor.

Maybe I can laugh about it after the new baby comes. Right now I'm too tired.

March 28, 1971

Happiness is—

Finding the missing sock in the wastebasket.

Getting both babies to sleep at the same time in the afternoon.

Getting another tooth cut.

Having the first baby trained before the third one arrives.

Sleeping three consecutive hours at night.

April 7, 1971

Ed's morale has been low with his present financial state. One attempt after another has failed and we vacillate from hope to discouragement, from grouchiness to good humor. He wants so much to succeed materially.

This week he is away in Jefferson City investigating a selling job. He is not a salesman, but keeps trying. My preference is for him to have a job, any job, just to make ends meet and raise a few cattle on the side, something James would even now enjoy watching. In a few years he would be helping. Ed is excellent with the children, a gentle loving father, and they love him. He's been a help to me during these last weeks especially, lifting them and babysitting occasionally.

Elizabeth seems to have a special warm spot for him and beams whenever he comes home. A sunshine girl, she has a sweet, placid disposition.

May 13, 1971

Our wee Michael John arrived April 23 about 10:30 a.m. I awoke early with backache and little subtle twinges which turned into a rhythm by 7:30—and they weren't quite so subtle then. I told James I was going to the hospital to get our new baby and he said, "No, too rainy and too cold." We looked at a book of baby Jesus and then I explained again that I was going to get *our* little baby and he could love and care for it. I'll never forget his smile. He and Mom waved us off. In our rush to leave we ran over friendly black tomcat. He was one of us, as Ed said.

Each baby is more fun to bring home. Elizabeth at fifteen months kept touching Michael and saying "baby" over and over with her beautiful smile. James came to the hospital with Ed to bring me home and was so proud. I hope he will remember this, but he's so young, just 28 months. One day he told me, "Mommy, the new baby's crying." Pause. "Mommy, he's yelling."

Ed is working part time at a nearby quarry. It's a help, but he isn't happy, and it's really not enough to support us anyway.

There seem to be threads of life, threads of joy, frustration and worry, prayer and trust, loneliness, all of them running parallel and simultaneous through each day. I am so very happy with my children; they are perfect in every way and I thank God for them daily. But along with this great joy, there is the thread of physical weariness, our financial dilemma, and the constant emotional drain of living with Grandma.

It's easy to complain. Some of my friends would gladly change places with me.

June 14, 1971

Rocking Michael till 12:30 a.m. Time to go around the world.

For all the folk in Pennsylvania I pray. I think of each dear one and wish I could see them more often. Bless Cherry especially, Lord, in her new marriage.

For Rosalind in England, her firstborn coming any day now. We have so much to share. Our "spirits blend around one common mercy seat."

For Hazel St. John getting the school through these last days of term in Beirut. All the heat and confusion, exams and graduation, the final time of sharing with the girls before they scatter to all parts of the Middle East. I can recall it vividly though it's far removed now.

For Una in Scotland, in love with Rory, as she does deputation to go to Aden and plans her marriage. Thank you, Lord, for all these years of rich friendship.

In South Africa Agnes de Smidt is keeping her active husband and family together in their home as they plan for the future and their return to Lebanon. Thank you for all she's meant to me.

For Joyce Karsen and hers in Taiwan. College mates and we've never met since then, yet the bonds of prayer hold us together in fellowship.

Lord, I'm so limited here in this little corner of Missouri. I'm so glad Your eyes run to and fro through the whole earth to show Yourself strong in behalf of those whose heart is perfect toward You.

June 23, 1971

At 1:00 a.m., drooping with sleepiness, I was feeding and rocking Michael. Three years of this nightly bottle-burp-rock routine has thoroughly exhausted me.

Ed rolled over, blinked, and said, "What'd you do, wake him up?" and went on sleeping.

Oh, sure, hubby, I always wake him at one. I miss him. Dear God, how much care they take.

July 18, 1971

This time I was making sure Elizabeth would damage nothing. Three grocery bags. I checked to see that all cookies, candy, and bread (she likes to squeeze it) were out of reach.

She was sitting in the backseat and James was standing behind me chirping into my ear about the cows and corn and trucks we passed. All was quiet with Elizabeth and I was pleased with my forethought. No paper rattling, no cookies spilled all over the floor.

As we pulled near the porch to unload babies and groceries, I looked back. There she was, finishing her project. She had quietly and efficiently peeled every banana and they were all turning into a miserable brown in the July heat. Mommy's little helper.

July 29, 1971

The babies are thriving. Michael, in spite of all his spitting up, is a fat good-natured little boy of three months who smiles at everyone. James said one day, "He wike me, Mommy, he *do*."

Elizabeth keeps life interesting. She loves the dog who obligingly shares his bones with her. When she gets hot, she sits in his water dish or a puddle, then waddles around with a great soggy diaper hanging down, or more likely, pulls it off and leaves it "out dere," pointing vaguely. Last week on a blistering hot day while I was canning and getting dinner, she poured a cup of ice water on Michael presumably to cool him off.

One day she gave me quite a fright. While rocking Michael, I realized I hadn't heard her for a while. I hurried outside and found her and Snowball far across the field headed straight toward the pond. Had she got there, I wouldn't have found her till too late.

She and James keep my prize geranium picked clean of the buds. They carefully pluck them and stick them in the sand—to grow flowers.

Who cares? I can't scold them. They are of more value than many flowers.

August 6, 1971

Lord, it's late and everyone's in bed. A good time to let the grouchiness and worry of the day slip off my back on to Yours. Thank You for my babies. I'm sorry when I get short-tempered and impatient. Bless all the small Pakistani hungry babies. Mine have everything and they have nothing.

From *Daily Light* a reminder. "The living God . . . giveth us richly all things to *enjoy.*" Even Grandma? I was cross again tonight. She is hard to enjoy. "My God shall supply all your need." I need thankfulness and love and patience and goodness. Supply my need according to your riches, Father.

August 29, 1971

Quite a day. Leonard Rodgers phoned about two and made visiting sounds. I invited them for supper and overnight. He said they'd arrive between five and six.

I got Michael to sleep and for half an hour helped Ed get his old tractor started. Made up beds and cots. Then James woke Michael and he had to be eased off again.

Uh-oh, no meat. I'll have to borrow from Wynona. She wasn't home, so Ben gave me four pounds of solid frozen hamburger. Hack it up, spread it out to thaw. I made potato salad, sliced tomatoes, mixed meat loaf, and baked a peach shortcake. Cleaned a little and was exhausted by 5:30.

Looking outside, I happened to see Grandma trip and fall on top of Elizabeth. Neither was hurt—they're both tough—but I was tired and scared and bawled. James said calmly, "Mommy, get a Kleenex." I sat to peel peaches and rest. Fat chance with a kid on either side yelling for peaches. Poor little souls; they must be hungry. When did we last eat?

I fed them, and still no Rodgers came. (They were lost). Set the table, feed Ed, bathe the babies. Finally they came and all the children ran in circles outside till ten while we gabbed about Beirut days. A great visit.

September 15, 1971

Lord, something's gone amiss. Maybe a whole lot of things. A quality of my life seems to have dried up, evaporated. The rituals of my faith are there, but the spirit has left. When?

Looking back, I know there has been no huge crisis or shattering calamity, just a mass of trivial things all piled up. Like James, I need "shomping else." Do You hear, Lord? Something besides crying babies, conniving to make ends meet, canning, catering to a lonely old woman—and failing miserably.

Grandma has ended up in a nursing home and I have to face the failure honestly. I keep thinking her other children could help with her, that Ed and I have done

68

enough, that my children need me first. All of which may be true, but I also know the love and joy of Christ have ebbed so low I have none to spare.

It's a sizzling September morning. Michael is still spitting up every hour or so and we both smell horrendously. Outside Elizabeth is likely looking for a mud puddle to jump into. Even my sense of humor is dried up.

But just now Agnes' letter has come from halfway round the world. "Maureen, don't forget joy."

Joy, that most positive of all Christian qualities. Sometimes I can pretend peace, even love, but joy is unmanageable unless the Source is there. Jesus had the audacity to talk of joy just hours before His own death. "I will see you again, and your heart shall rejoice, and your joy no man taketh from you." Profound promises of joy in the face of Gethsemane.

There is a part of every person that can be filled only with Christ. When He is crowded out, nothing quite compensates. And when He is there, nothing else matters. As Paul put it in Colossians, "You have everything when you have Christ."

Everything?

That's a big order, Father. I'm waiting.

"HE RESTORETH MY SOUL: HE LEADETH ME IN THE PATHS OF RIGHTEOUSNESS FOR HIS NAME'S SAKE."

God's leading—how remarkable. This time it was back to Narvon where I'd been brought so often to restore my soul.

Travel this path of righteousness with me to family stability and growth, to hard work and unexpected rewards, to encouragement and peace of mind.

CHAPTER 4

AMAZING GRACE

September 25, 1971

We have leased the land for ten years to a neighbor. That is a great burden gone. To leave it idle is not possible financially. Taxes and interest go on. Ed doesn't think he can make a living by farming, so he felt this was best. I do too. It is one less thing to worry about, though I'm disappointed that farming has not worked out.

We're tossing other thoughts around, even that I might go back to teaching again if I can get a job. I have always said I would not work while the children are small and lose these early years with them. On the other hand we have to face reality. If we could live in Pennsylvania near my parents, we would have babysitters who truly loved them. That would make it easier for me to leave them. For months Ed has been talking about moving where there is more opportunity.

November 7, 1971

After many ups and downs, we *are* going to Pennsylvania. I've been tired and tense and Ed is not sure about the move at all. But a strange thing happened, almost a miracle. The house across the road from Mom and Dad is newly vacated and we will rent it. It's old, a comedown from this lovely modern house, but quite adequate. It will be fun to paper and paint and make it homelike. There's a huge lawn, lots of room for the children to play in.

Yet I've felt no elation at all about going. We seem to have had so many discouragements and setbacks and misunderstandings. Grandma is in the nursing home. We had planned to take her along to Pennsylvania where she could live in a small apartment near our home, eat with us as before, and see our children daily. Without all the other pressures we've had, I feel I could cope. However, none of her other children want her to go, so we probably can't do it.

We both feel drained and disappointed after so many failures. I keep praying that we'll get along better in a new place and that Ed will like it.

November 20, 1971

During naps and at night I managed to pack all my china in boxes, carefully with paper, each piece secure. In the guest room I hid them, so the babies wouldn't find them.

They did anyway. One day I realized they had been unusually quiet for a while and I walked down the hall. The door was shut but within I heard great rattles and clicks. There James and Elizabeth had a tea party set on the twin bed with my bone china cups. They were busily shaking salt and pepper all over the white bedspreads.

How does one pack and move 1,200 miles with three babies all under age three?

December 16, 1971

Thank God for families. Dad and Russ roared out during the Thanksgiving holidays and helped us move. Ed drove the farm truck loaded heavily with our possessions and Dad followed him. Russ took the babies and me in the car which developed a problem about midnight, thwarting our plans to drive straight through. We took a motel room and waited to get it repaired in the morning. My funny, inquisitive children were delighted and explored every nook for several hours before I got them settled. I never knew babies could sleep so little as mine do.

Stopping for a meal, we lost Elizabeth briefly. Russ had carried her in barefooted—her favorite project is taking off her shoes. I dashed around the restaurant and found her placidly sitting with woolly coat and bare feet beside an admiring truck driver on his way to California.

Christmas is in the air, the house finally in some kind of order, Ed with a job, and I am unwinding a little. I hope I get a little sweeter again. I seem to have been tense and grouchy a long time.

January 25, 1972

Two years ago my beautiful baby girl was born. She's such a darling. They waved me off to school this morning and I cried a little because I was leaving them. That is the only ache in teaching again. I've had two days of substituting and the prospect of much more. It's a real lift financially, but I've had to rearrange my notions of motherhood.

Michael has four teeth after many struggles, and he walks around the couch now. He smiles so much, our little PR man.

March 4, 1972

A super surprise this week. A letter from Dr. Wirt of *Decision* asking me to write another article for them! He wants the story of our romance included in a general testimony. So I must get busy. No brainstorms yet, but as I work and write, ideas will come. I seem to be frantically busy these days at school and at home.

I've been sifting and sorting, trying to get meaning out of some of the experiences of these last years. It will help my writing if I can, and me as well.

May 8, 1972

I am so stunned. I learned today that Jean Boyer° is on drugs, LSD no less. I keep thinking of how I've been too busy to phone her, to visit, to pay special attention. She has always been irresponsible, hard to pin down for a visit, and I've excused myself. But the extra mile might have helped. I can't think now what to do but must try to see her. And pray.

How little we know of each other's burdens.

May 13, 1972

Hubby is working the third shift, an unpleasant dreary time to go to work.

His heart for animals is very soft. He found a stray cat the other night and carried it home (dropping and break-

---

° fictitious name

ing his new thermos to do it). I found Calico on the doorstep next morning feeling quite at home.

Elizabeth has adopted "Sally Read," as she calls it, and it is a remarkably patient creature indeed. She holds it with great determination, but little concern which end is up. I suppose Sally can sense love.

June 4, 1972

The hill is bereft of menfolk. Dad has had back surgery after some miserable weeks. One realizes how vulnerable he is, as we all are.

Ed has gone to Missouri to see his mother and while there has painted the house and run errands. He so much wants to be a success. I hope this trip refreshes him.

With our babies how could we be poor? Michael, standing, trying to walk, falling, laughing. The conversations of Elizabeth and James are priceless. She said to him one day, "I hear a motorcycle." He told me, "She's pulling my weg." Which she often does. James has learned some Bible verses and both of them go around singing "Amazing Grace" at the top of their voices.

The other day Elizabeth asked a question. When I answered her, she said very pointedly, "I'm talking to James." The perfect squelch.

They are our treasures.

June 18, 1972

So tired I can hardly move. While the menfolk are gone, I cut both lawns, no mean task. They're huge. Melissa and Sylvia have been here each day until five when Peg gets them. Tonight I had hot dogs and strawberry shortcake for all of them plus Mom who's been running back and forth to the hospital so much.

Baths and bedtime are always busy, but this evening was chaotic. In an effort to put old records away and new ones on, we spilled a bouquet of flowers all over the stereo. (*Why* do I try to cultivate a love of music on hot nights?) James bawled. He thought we'd ruined it. I did too. While I got Elizabeth to bed, Michael tipped over in the armchair which I had pulled out when wiping up. Both boys cried. James to bed. I lay down and Michael romped over me till he eventually wore down.

Now a cup of tea.

June 27, 1972

"Faithful are the wounds of a friend." Recently Ed reminded me that I've been yelling at the children too much. They are so young, babies in fact, and I should be a little quieter and more patient with them. I responded by telling him quite loudly that *he* wasn't with them all day and all night and he yelled too and furthermore he— Then I realized what I was doing and turned tearful and reproachful.

He's right, though, and I finally had to admit it to him. Raising one's voice is a habit and loses its effect when used too much, not to mention hurt feelings and constant tension around the house.

July 7, 1972

This morning little James, age 3½, with eyes shining said suddenly, "Mommy, I can hardly wait to see Jesus." Uh, yes, that will be nice, won't it, James?

"Are you sure He's up there? I wanta see Him, Mommy." Had he noticed my hesitation? Yes, little feller, He's up there and He must love to hear you say that. And I want to see Him too, only not yet, not yet. Life is so sweet and babies so dear.

August 15, 1972

During the hottest week of summer, I decided it was time to start overhauling and rearranging the house. Much to Ed's horror, I got wallpaper and began on the big room upstairs that had been a junkroom. I was tired of running up and down half a dozen times a night to check on various calls, cries, and thumps (Elizabeth falling out of bed). Ed and I could certainly sleep upstairs where I would hear and see easier. But first it had to be made habitable.

It was a *big effort*. For one thing, in spite of the heat, the door had to be kept shut when working so Michael wouldn't fall down the steps. Oh yes, all three helped. They ate the paste and snipped up the wallpaper and kept losing the tape measure and rollers. Elizabeth cut off the hair on her right side and now has a very naked ear. James did his usual constant chirping, wanting so hard to help, and kept me thoroughly confounded as I matched flowers and measured windows.

It took a whole week to do that one room but it turned out beautifully. That was the first step. I bought a piece of linoleum for a cheap nine dollars and stuck it in the car and told the kids not to move. Well, the linoleum rolled up and down the window ledge with every swerve of the car, and the kids complained that it hit them in the face and they couldn't see over it. We made it home slowly. Ed stared in amazement, then helped me carry it upstairs, shaking his head over the foibles of his wife.

There were many more steps, but we're sleeping in the room now. I'm pleased and very exhausted.

August 24, 1972

I persuaded Ed to bring some "junk," as he termed it, from Peg's. One was an old rickety table that I told him brightly would be just fine if he put in a bolt or two. He did and it is.

The other is my special pride, a china cupboard. I've been antiquing it at night after the children are in bed. "Midnight madness," Ed calls it. It has turned out astonishingly handsome. Now I have the great pleasure of putting my pretty dishes, silver pieces, and souvenirs from various countries into it.

Several turbulent weeks later and we have a new bedroom, a rather charming one if I do say so, and a dining room/family room. I can actually invite people to eat with us. We feel much more spacious.

Even hubby is amazed at the results.

August 27, 1972

The prayers at our table are so comical and so solemn that I never know whether to laugh or cry. James tries to say everything Ed says, interrupting loudly when he forgets—"Rex and Jean, the Tuckeys, Jerry Weldy, health and strength. ..." Elizabeth closes her eyes tightly and whispers to herself. Michael makes a fat clasp and mumbles a little jumble.

I watch.

One night we had just a can of pork and beans for supper. After the brief grace, James said, "A short prayer for a short meal."

September 8, 1972

Elizabeth has a really healthy appetite. One morning I made two soft-boiled eggs for her and James. She soon had hers eaten and then gobbled up his as well.

As he came downstairs she said with a wicked gleam, "I ate your egg." He threw a little fit which is what she wanted. Says she coyly, "I like you, James."

September 24, 1972

It was the first day I was called back to school this year. The teacher whom I was replacing was a discontented young woman, not profound but extremely pronounced in her views. As to religion, she was a cynic, possibly an agnostic.

That was the astonishing part, the courage of her students in being willing to speak up. The class was to sit in a circle and each student individually give his ideal or goal in life. Only a few were able to speak on this particular day, but from each class I heard at least one give a distinctly Christian goal.

One tall boy, obviously a leader, said the Bible was the most important thing to him and he believed it, all of it. When questioned, he spoke quietly yet forcefully. A girl introduced her talk by saying she knew a lot of kids would misunderstand and criticize her. She had many faults and she didn't want them to think she was trying to be pious or perfect. Nevertheless, she was a follower of Christ, He had died for her, and she loved Him.

None of them were ridiculed, at least not in class. The others listened, questioned them closely, respected their viewpoint.

Their teacher-for-a-day returned home amazed and

thanking God that a few students in a modern high school valued Christ enough to publicly speak for Him even in a classroom where the teacher normally mocked anything old-fashioned or Christian.

God must have a very warm heart toward these youngsters.

November 28, 1972

Kids. You can break your heart for love of them and the next minute hold your sides with laughter. Various remarks heard at our house lately:

James on the way home from the doctor, "Mommy, if you go to heaven, I want to go too." Especially poignant as he could hardly breathe from his cold. He has had so much croup all his life.

Elizabeth in the car, talking as she often did about breaking her head, "If I break my head, then I be with Jesus till Mommy and Daddy come."

Another day, to vary their favorite hymn, she sang cheerfully, "Amazing grace! how sweet the sound that saved a wretch like —Mommy." I smiled tolerantly. It was true.

I put some candles on the windowsill and the first night Michael, full of wonder, went over and admired them. I'll never forget that wee head and fat arms reaching up to the light.

December 7, 1972

Today complimentary copies of *Decision* came with my story "Amazing Grace." As always, it is a unique thrill to see oneself in print. I've been getting fan letters for three weeks now which was tantalizing when I hadn't seen the article myself. It turned out to be a wild morning of washing sheets, making cookies, dinner, kids, and I couldn't even read it when it came.

Ed and I were married five years on December 2. No special celebration but a lovely quiet evening with our children. And he read Proverbs 31 to me again.

December 25, 1972

Christmas. Is there a day like it? A thousand images and memories are conjured up with the word.

Around the tree this morning there was great excitement. Elizabeth got her doll she planned on and could hardly get round to the rest. Finally she did and a little coach entranced her as well as the boys. James' packages were ripped open in minutes. The best was a "bulbozer" as they call it. Fat Michael just sat and soaked up all kinds of peace and good will.

Dinner for seventeen, including assorted childless aunts and uncles who love to be with children, Mom and Dad, Russ and his family. Grandma Read was alone in Missouri. I wish often she lived near us and could join in these happy times.

We sang carols this afternoon. Elizabeth has begged to be Mary so I dressed her in her housecoat and a blue scarf that matched her eyes. A beautiful little madonna with her new doll. James, dressed as Joseph, sang with her "Away in a Manger" and the "Friendly Beasts."

"MY CUP RUNNETH OVER."

During the lovely interlude I'm about to share with you I was happier than I had ever been in my life. The children were past the woes and weariness of babyhood and I was satisfyingly busy in caring for them. It would not last, but I would always look back with nostalgia on this cup of joy that was ours and running over.

Enjoy with me these gifts of life and love, everything He gave me.

CHAPTER 5

I LOVE EVERYTHING YOU GAVE ME

January 1, 1973

Sitting in my former church last night at the New Year's Eve service, I glanced around at old friends. Many were truly old now and I noted again the steady aging that imperceptibly goes on all the time, yet hits one with staggering abruptness after a space of several years of absence.

From the back the voices of the choir began lightly, distantly, growing steadily louder and fuller as they walked down the aisle singing.

I have decided to follow Jesus,
I have decided to follow Jesus,
I have decided to follow Jesus,
No turning back, no turning back.

There *is* no turning back. With force I realized it again, that one can never follow Jesus and be the same again. The very quality of life has been changed and one is never quite able to forget Him.

87

I knew. I had tried, but His voice pulled me back each time.

In college I wanted to follow the call of love. I tried to be sophisticated and believe that a rendezvous on the stairs or on the campus lawn was the light of each day. In summer I waited for his letters and my day rose and fell with the arrival of the mail. Yet with all the persuasive words of my boyfriend, his persistent, masculine logic that love was the only thing that mattered, in the background I kept hearing *Him*. He had withdrawn Himself but left echoes of clear laughter, bright dreams, and beauty without blemish that made my love a paltry thing.

Along the way I tried to turn to intellectual satisfaction. Somehow Christ seemed so simple. Kierkegaard, Plato, Camus, Waugh—men like these—I read and thought over and talked about. "All is vanity," said the preacher. A dimension was missing and I was always searching for wholeness.

Turning then to myself, I was sure that with my maturity and good sense, I could manipulate and handle life, most of the time anyway. But somehow the wear and tear of countless small worries, the weariness of babies and bottles, diapers and dishes, the heat and loneliness broke my spirit. The nagging constant problem of daily living sapped me more than a great calamity would have. Then I heard again those lovely words, "Come unto me, all ye that labour and are heavy laden, and I will give you rest."

I had decided to follow Jesus many years before and there was no turning back. Not now or ever. There at Calvary Church, old friends brought back old memories, decisions, paths. And that familiar voice, forever new and winsome and fresh, saying, "Follow me."

January 17, 1973

It was evening after a long day. It had been rough in school, and then my own three seemed to be fighting all evening. Ed was at work.

Now it was bedtime. Just the milk . . . and cookies routine and I would get them in one by one. What was that on the top of the cupboard? A coffee can. It must be some cookies sent up by Aunt Sadie with the kids today. I grabbed it and a can of greasy diesel fuel splashed over my clothes, into all the crevices of the cupboard, and on the floor. Michael started crying. I did too.

Hot soapy water to clean the floor. Give the cupboard a cursory swipe. It would take hours to clean properly. Change clothes and do a load of hot wash.

The place still smelled.

How can a husband put diesel fuel in the kitchen? In a coffee can on top of a cupboard? What's a garage for?

When Ed came home from work at 11:30, I heard him chuckling up the stairs. By then my own sense of humor was stirring, but I wouldn't let him know it. Stop laughing or I'll kick you out of bed.

February 15, 1973

We passed two more birthdays in January again. It's always a gala time. James gets very excited while Elizabeth calmly enjoys it. The chief thing she remembered about hers was "I had pink icing," as she told a little friend.

She had chicken pox quite severely and was miserable

a few days, the only time she has ever been sick. I came home from school one day when Mom was with her. She was flushed with fever and her eyes were enormous. "Mommy, I like the taste of you best."

February 25, 1973

These evenings I am busy writing a chapter for the third edition of *Live Coal from the Altar*. Ken Campbell asked me to do it as "Reflections of a Friend." It is years since Alice was killed so suddenly, yet she has seemed to live with me as I wrote, especially the year we were roommates. There are some difficult things in this life that only in the next life will we understand. Her death is one of them.

I've started an evening Bible study for neighbor women. Jane candidly admitted she's an agnostic, but willing to come. So far she's been the most regular. We're studying Mark.

March 12, 1973

Through the night, when I woke, I had dreaded the next day—and prayed. Classes for this particular teacher were wild. A collection of smart aleck ninth-graders. Two boys in particular had caused me grief. Rude, arrogant, never embarrassed by anything I could say or do to them. It's hard to cope with youngsters who have no respect, worse when I don't even know their names.

Then strangely, inexplicably, I found them quiet, busy in their research assignment. Did my prayers help? Maybe I need to pray more for the hassles of *every* day, the trivial nagging problems that strain my spirit and drain my energy.

March 20, 1973

"Tell me a story, Grampie."

So Grampie, a tireless Irish storyteller, began. He told of Jacob pillowed on a stone watching the angels climbing the ladder.

"Tell me another story."

There was Daniel and the lions. Then the baby Moses and Joseph with his many-colored coat. Hoping finally to satisfy little James, Grampie began the story of the plagues of Egypt. Locusts and frogs and flies, sick cows and lice and water turned to blood. With the unselfconscious honesty of small children, James slid off the couch.

"That's too long," he said walking off.

Perfectly guileless.

April 28, 1973

What is sweeter than a little girl with a flower? There was Elizabeth bent over a humble dandelion. She looks carefully, plucks, and sniffs delicately. Tightly held in fat fist, she carries it to me, talking softly all the time. A present for Mommy. Pure gold.

May 1, 1973

Leisurely frying bacon, I reflected happily that all the schools must have bypassed me that day. It was too beautiful a day to be in school anyway. The children and I would work in the garden.

At five minutes to eight the phone rang. Would I be librarian for the day? Librarian? Okay, I'll go.

The bacon was rather wizened by now and my little ones started straggling downstairs. Both they and I were out of the notion of my teaching that day. Eventually I got the bacon and eggs on the table, Michael's bottle and fu-fu (diaper) for him.

My clothes changed, I started to find something for the children to wear. Michael had one of his out-of-sorts mornings. He kept hanging on me to "wead" his book. When Grammie appeared, he finally let loose of me, and I tried to get out the door.

Not so easily. Elizabeth began to cry. "I don't want an egg. I want Lucky Charms." I rushed back. Oh, my, ants in the Charms. Oh, well, they looked clean. Sift out the ants and eat the cereal anyway.

I left with cries of "Bye, Mommy" and a sigh on my part that a beautiful day was to be spent in school.

May 8, 1973

For the first time I wasn't teaching on a Tuesday when I had Bible study in the evening. In the morning I baked a luscious-looking marble cake as a sort of extra treat for tea afterward.

The kitchen floor was washed and waxed. It *smelled* clean. The whole house was dusted and vacuumed, a gold Damascus cloth on the dining room table. A couple hundred toys and clothes picked up. The place looked great.

Then Nancy phoned. She had company coming. Jane's husband was late and she couldn't leave the kids. Sue had previous plans. No one else bothered to call. No one came.

Lord, it's hard to persist, insist on having a Bible study when no one is able to come. Everyone is so busy, or tied down, legitimately for the most part. Am I to go on? Can one try too hard?

May 15, 1973

I did try again. Jane and Marian came to Bible Study. It was Marian's first time and she seemed to enjoy it. We studied Mark 3. Ordinary words but edged with eternity. "A house divided against itself cannot stand. . . . He that shall blaspheme against the Holy Ghost is in danger of eternal damnation. . . . Whosoever shall do the will of God, the same is my brother, and my sister, and mother."

Doing the will of God. That's the whole point of the Christian faith. "He that doeth the will of God abideth *forever*." Did they see it? Our session was very ordinary, spiced with anecdotes about Abraham Lincoln and our children and women's lib. Yet those eternal words live on and go with them. With Jane, agnostic but with an alert mind seeking, sifting, occasionally laughing at the turn of a phrase or an unsettling miracle. With Marian, unchurched but aware of her lack, not sure what she wants.

They liked the tea and brownies. Do they like Christ a little better than before?

May 17, 1973

He was a good-looking boy. Deep brown eyes and a bright face with a smile lurking in it. As I walked into the room, he eyed me, sized me up, and planned his tactics.

While I sat at the desk writing busily, my schoolteacher antenna began to warn me. That boy was up to mischief. His hands were hidden on his lap, but they were moving, cutting something. As I walked quickly back to his desk, he slammed whatever he had into the desk.

"What were you cutting?"

"Nuthin'."

"Let me see what you were cutting."

"Just a book cover. Nuthin' much." He showed me.
What did you use?"

"My fingernail."

"*Give me your knife.*"

The boy was terrified. "Please, I can't give it to you.
I'll get expelled. I've been in a lotta trouble. Mr. Jordan
said he'd expel me if I was sent to him again."

"Give it to me."

At the end of the period he begged another five
minutes for the return of the knife, for mercy. The brown
eyes were wet now. I said I'd talk to him after school. He
came, the shining face looking hopefully at me.

"Look, boy, I want to tell you something. Jesus loves
you. He loves you more than anyone else does. He
doesn't want you getting into trouble. You pray, kid, and
He'll help you. Here's your knife. Take it home and keep
it there. I want you to remember what I've said every
time you look at it—that Someone loves you."

"I know," he said "I will; thanks a lot."

His face was bright as he rushed off to his bus. "While
we were yet sinners, Christ died for us."

Mercy.

May 23, 1973

The sweetest time of the day is surely after they are in
bed and I go from one to the other checking the windows
and straightening a blanket.

Michael, his fat fingers curled, thoroughly round and
innocent, is still a baby. Two years old but how he loves
bottles and laps. Lord, he has such a lovely smile. Thank
you for my friendly boy. I hope he always likes people.

And Lord, maybe You could arrange for him to sleep through the night. I'd like that for a change.

My little girl. Sleep enhances her vivid coloring, the curls are tumbled, and she is all that I ever wanted in a daughter. I hope she keeps her present equanimity and good sense. She is so competent. Lord, may she use that quality in *helping*.

James with arms flung over his head. Always taking so much of my energy and effort, yet the most sensitive. Dear God, give him wisdom and stability. With his natural thoughtfulness he will be a great man.

I linger. And Lord, remember all the little ones who have no mommy to tuck them in.

June 2, 1973

It was quite a night and a day. Melissa and Sylvia came to spend the night since Ed is in Missouri again. I put all five in bed at the same time and hoped for the best. It sounded pretty good so long as I was busy in the kitchen, but when I sat down with the paper, I began to hear whispers, coughs, snores, giggles, all punctuated with occasional shouts and chirps from Michael who was being royally entertained. For over an hour I rumbled and roared now and again and eventually they went to sleep.

The night was bumpy. Six people in two rooms with one or more waking every hour or two.

They all seemed ready to get up before I did.

Five children, three pets, and forty or fifty ants for breakfast. The remarkable thing is that the more children one has, the more they do for themselves. I think.

I shooed them out the door and they swarmed around

the old pickup sitting out front for our transportation while Ed is gone. It was the best plaything we ever had. They set up housekeeping in the truck bed and stayed there most of the day. I gave them sandwiches and Kool-Aid for lunch and took a nap while they played on.

June 30, 1973

How quickly they grow. Michael says a lot now including "Flip-flep" for Elizabeth. He also joins in the nightly bedside prayers. "Unta pray," he says. Last night he rushed in beside us with his little yellow hard hat on. The Father must have smiled to see this small boy with sturdy hard hat bowed gravely, murmuring his devotions.

Yet in the morning they're all babies and I sit and cuddle each one awhile as they get up. James said to me one day, "I like your lap a lot, Mommy."

July 28, 1973

Menu for meditation: Take one hot July morning. Quickly do breakfast dishes and two loads of wash. Find the coolest possible clothes for three restless children. Lead them unobtrusively out of the house and under a tree. Remark on the wonders of their trucks and dog. Pet the dog. Return surreptitiously to the house. Set up the fan and get a glass of iced tea. Sit down and *think*.

August 9, 1973

Sweltering heat these days. I should *not* be trying special projects. Today I ruined completely, irreparably, ten dollars worth of dress material. Just miscalculated, slashed, and it was done. Hmph, I guess I have to admit what I've always known. I am not a really good seamstress.

Edward H. and Maureen Hay Read (Decision photo by Ake Lundberg)

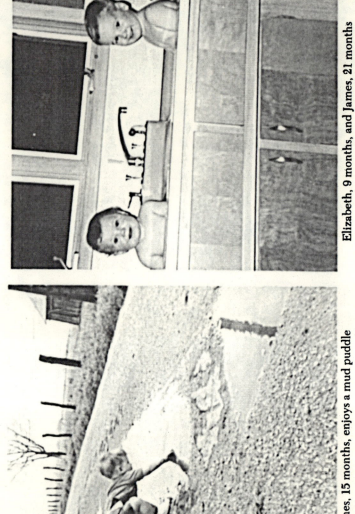

Elizabeth, 9 months, and James, 21 months

James, 15 months, enjoys a mud puddle

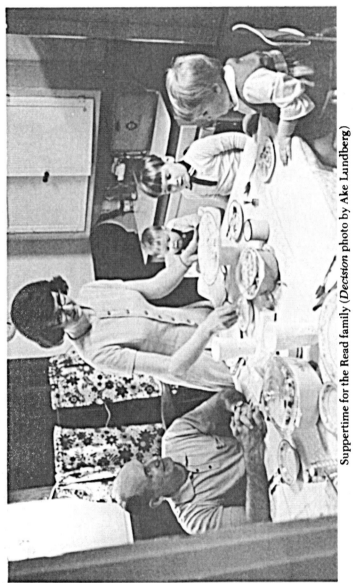

Suppertime for the Read family (*Decision* photo by Ake Lundberg)

Michael, Maureen, James, Ed, and Elizabeth (*Decision* photo by Ake Lundberg)

Elizabeth at 3½

Michael at 4½

James, Michael, and Elizabeth, Christmas 1973

Michael, 4½, James, 7, and Susan, 6½

James Read, 7 years old

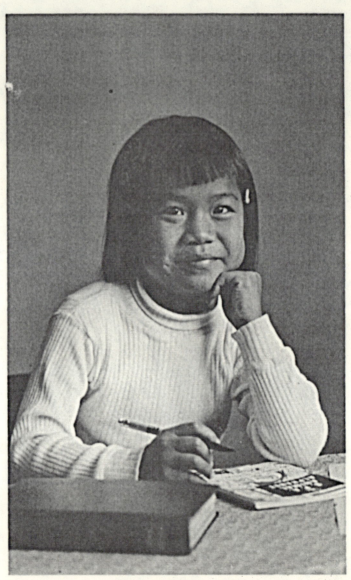

Susan Read, 6½ years old

Marie and Dewey McConaghay have been having their own Gethsemane with their family. The suffering they have known never makes any sense. And through it all, Marie keeps smiling. Maybe God gave her to people like me to show what grace under pressure really means, that with Christ one can triumph.

I have vague hopes of going to Europe! Dad and Mom put money aside some years ago for Russ and me and our spouses to take a trip. Russ and Peg have gone this summer to Spain and France, and I have really got the fever to see all my friends again.

August 15, 1973

Last Saturday we five sneaked off to a youth rally hoping none of our more conservative friends would see us and be alarmed. We were impressed. Those young people were orderly, neat, happy, and sharing love with everyone. Even with stodgy old folks like us.

As we arrived in a beginning thunderstorm, we looked down over thousands of kids singing with arms upraised, "Praise the Lord. Praise the Lord. Praise the Lord" in a beautiful chant. Within minutes the cloud above us split, the rain stopped and clear light shone through.

The speaker seemed rather demonstrative, emotional to my taste, but after all a converted drug addict and gang leader has reason to be excited about the gospel. How could I begin to know his past, or his present either for that matter? No two of us are alike, but all members of the same body of Christ and we need each other.

Our little ones were squirming and we had to leave before the end. But then I hope there was no end. I'm praying those kids are on their way home still praising

God for the rain, still smiling, still exuberantly loving Jesus.

I've wondered since, *was* it excessive? But then, was David excessive when he cried out, "Bless the Lord, O my soul: and all that is within me, bless his holy name!" Was Ezra too demonstrative when he led the Israelites to worship "and all the people answered, Amen, Amen, with lifting up their hands and they bowed their heads, and worshipped the Lord with their faces to the ground"? Was Saul, later Paul, too emotional when he fell to the earth and said trembling, "Lord, what wilt thou have me to do?" Or how about the verse in Job that says "the morning stars sang together and all the sons of God shouted for joy?"

I wonder if God, just to show He is still alive and working, decided to take this restless generation and prove again that His Son can redeem. I wonder if He wanted especially to gather some from the hopeless, drug-addicted, sex-oriented, lonely confused kids to Himself. If so, who are we to criticize?

August 20, 1973

We have so much. Three beautiful children for whom many would give all their money. Health for each of us. Friends, what wealth they are. And Jesus, He is ours.

Tonight the katydids are singing merrily, tunelessly. Zinnias, brilliant and sturdy on the table, Tchaikovsky's 49th on the radio, the dampness from the storm soaking into flowers, tomatoes, and corn in the garden, in the black sky a nearly whole moon glowing orange and benevolent. Surrounded by riches.

Our deaf neighbor or the little crippled boy over the

106

hill would trade with us any day.

Lord, help us to be thankful just for what we have. Help us to see it, to listen, to taste. Help us, help me to be open to new experiences if that's Your will, but also to see and know the new that is in every single day. Help us to be *alive*.

August 23, 1973

At bedtime little James said he wanted Jesus to come and forgive his sins and live with him, for always. He insisted we pray together, and he went to sleep tonight rejoicing.

The simplicity of it struck me. The God of the universe can be called on by one small boy just four-and-a-half or a great sinner of eighty. It requires one thing, faith in Jesus. "For there is none other name under heaven given among men, whereby we must be saved." The name of Jesus. So limiting, the only way, yet so wide it includes whosoever will.

Sometimes James prays aloud when he's up in bed. The other evening I overheard and wrote quickly—

Dear Jesus,
Thank you for the food and water and my milk You gave me.
I pray for Uncle Russ and Aunt Peg and Missy and Sylvia and Scott and Mark away over in Africa and Tracy and Angie.
Thank you for the church You gave us and for our house.
I love everything You gave me.
I close in Jesus' name. Amen.

September 13, 1973

Jeremiah was told not to be afraid of men's faces. I

have to tell myself over and over not to be afraid of the faces of a roomful of teenagers.

Walking into a classroom, especially if the day has already begun, is always an act of courage for me. The kids snicker, comment, whistle sardonically, *react*. A substitute is fair game. I am middle-aged, conservative, and my dress is at least five years old. They are the now generation. How can I possibly teach or reach them? I note beards, palazzo pants, platform shoes, the unbecoming mixtures of stripes and colors. What ugly styles. Or is it that I'm just too set in my memories of the fifies?

We watch each other warily. Overheard remarks: What do we have next? Me and my old man don't get along. Hey, let's knock off Sullivan's class. He's not here today. Say, did you see the game? All interspersed with some colorful obscenities.

They're not a whole lot different from kids of ten or fifteen years ago in one way. In another, there's a hardness, a sophistication that should have been postponed. They're too young to be so cynical, so—so realistic.

How could I get through? How do I get across to them that I'm not out to make life miserable for them, that I like kids, that I once was exactly where they are? I know their insecurity, their strange sense of humor, the emotional excesses, their boundless energy, their dreams.

Jesus loves them, but He's not here. Only I'm here. I've got to love them for Him. That's the only thing that can penetrate their hardness, frivolity, sophistication. Love never fails.

September 24, 1973
So often I have wondered how I can ever prepare my

108

children for *all* the problems, tragedies, disappointments, and just the sheer drabness of so much of life. How can I get my sensitive James to know how brutal school life is, for example? All the ridicule, fights, jealousy, plain meanness that make up a school year? And how will I ever keep Elizabeth from conceit over her loveliness and warn her of the bitterness and envy that follow a beautiful woman? The insincere flattery that a man can give her? Suppose she lost her pretty face for some reason? And how will this tender little Michael be able to face the brutality of war, accidents, crime, death?

I think of terrible sickness they can face, the worries and problems of unsuitable marriages, the possibilities of having retarded children, crippling accidents, loneliness.

How does one give them the wisdom, the patience, the will to cope with all this?

"Train up a child in the way he should go." Yes, Lord, but *how?* I would drive them to distraction, make them fearful and timid if I tried to explain all the possibilities and probabilities of life. What principle can I get across to them that will stand them in every situation?

That beautiful word comes to mind—*trust*. "Trust in the Lord with all thine heart." "Thou wilt keep him in perfect peace, whose mind is stayed on thee: because he trusteth in thee." "What time I am afraid, I will trust in thee."

If they learn to trust Him in everything—sickness, disaster, death, and also in success and happiness—that will carry them through. Trust gives perspective, a sense of proportion, peace. It keeps one from centering on oneself. There are too many trials that bankrupt one. A bigger Person is needed.

I know, Lord. I've found it so. Now help me to trust you for *their* futures.

October 5, 1973

Out of the mouth of babes. . . .

Last night Elizabeth and Michael were sitting on the piano bench making a joyful noise. Elizabeth put her arm around him and said, "I like you, Michael." Said he to her, "Me wike oo, too!"

Elizabeth seems to have been given wisdom and insight beyond her years. To Ed she said one day, "Daddy, you know I'm just a little girl, and if you don't pick me up, it will make me very nervous." He picked her up.

We had quite a happening in the doll family. Several days ago Elizabeth was crying and told me with tears that her baby died and went to heaven. Michael walked about saying woefully, "Ba-by died." A few days later I asked how she was feeling by now. She said quite philosophically, "Well, that's just the way life is."

October 10, 1973

We're playing Christmas records these days at our house. Too early? To restrict our celebration of the greatest gift to a few days in December is impossible, almost an insult. We savor the season as long as possible.

The children and I always have months of preparation. James especially must have inherited my love for this favorite season. We make decorations, plan our company, our cookies, make more decorations, listen to records, and learn the words.

Christmas comes at the most appropriate time of year

when the days are shortest, nights long and black. Into this gloom comes all the splash of reds and golds, stars and bells, smells of cakes and cookies, secrets, surprises, and a gradual renewing sense of the immense love of God who "spared not his own Son, but delivered him up for us all." Delivered Him from the body of a humble woman to the cruelty of the cross. The glitter of Christmas hides this, unless one takes the time to remember. But there's joy in this season, and what Christian virtue is greater than joy? Joy that no man can take away.

"Joy to the world, the Lord is come!"

October 26, 1973

When I am old and lonely and sad, I shall look back at my present life with nostalgia and longing. For even now I know that these are probably the happiest years I shall have with my children.

The worry and furious work of infancy is past and I have finally graduated from diapers and teething, spitting up and nightly feedings to the relative calm of spilled milk and play dough all over the carpet.

These are small problems. For there are also wonderful walks through the woods with my youngsters as we gather orange leaves and look at blue sky. Our dog races energetically around us.

And we have long evenings when we sit around the table and trace out wreaths and bells and stars. A little paste and glitter give them some glamor. James piles them carefully in a drawer to be hung at Christmas.

Story time is every evening. We look at Michael's fire engine book or farm animals, then I ease him off to bed.

James and Elizabeth are ready for the new Bible story books. We're in volume seven, the parables of Christ. I realize again what a master storyteller Jesus was. Even a four-year-old loves them. What an enrichment the Bible is to a child, to me.

Working in the garden planting bulbs is another lesson in faith, putting that dry, wrinkled brown bulb into the earth and waiting expectantly for the melody of color next spring. Brilliant daffodils, a huddle of cheerful crocuses, graceful tulip cups. The children get so excited about "pitty fouders" as Michael calls them.

If and when I am 85, my scrapbook of memories will be often looked at and shared. I shall, no doubt, be pesky and a burden to someone. I shall worry people with old stories, old memories. But I shall be warmed and comforted with what once was mine.

December 6, 1973

She cuddled up tight against me in church and leaned her head on my sleeve. I patted her hand and she gripped it hard. Looking at her, I realized suddenly how long she had grown. Three-almost-four Elizabeth was a little girl, not a baby, and I wondered how she had slid over infancy so fast.

She is the middle child and somehow her brothers have crowded her. Her own natural independence made her sufficient so early and she has slipped quietly into girlhood. Blessed with a placid contentment, she has seldom troubled me. I can still see her sitting in her infant chair smiling whenever anyone walked past. And I remember her in the first pink dress she wore, a beautiful, golden-haired little girl, the kind I wanted since I was ten. She was thoroughly feminine, and unconsciously naughty. There was the day I found her in the corner slurping up a rotten apple, and the time she dragged toilet paper all over the house, unwinding as she went. When she rubbed Vaseline into her hair, she told me she was putting on "me-cine." I spent three days trying to get it out.

No more. Those days are gone. Now she likes to help me make brownies and looks after Michael.

Little daughter, nestled warm against me, I'm cherishing each moment. How soon you'll be wearing your first makeup. You'll giggle and write notes and ice skate and fall in love. You'll learn to drive, go to college, dream dreams, and marry.

But for now you are here. I love you.

December 24, 1973 (Christmas Eve)

I shall always remember my children's faces by candlelight. Dressed up in their best clothes, they ran from room to room admiring the candles and our beautiful big tree with its new extra string of lights. The table was full of goodies. The clan started to gather and we had a memorable evening.

"God is light, and in him is no darkness at all." That light has pierced through the ages and reached us again tonight.

"YEA, THOUGH I WALK THROUGH THE
VALLEY OF THE SHADOW OF DEATH,
I WILL FEAR NO EVIL: FOR
THOU ART WITH ME."

*Into this valley God abruptly led, and for a
time I could see nothing but shadows and sorrow.
I floundered, fainted, fell, but sensed dimly His
glory and eternal love as He lifted me and led me
back to faith and hope.*

*Come over this somber path and recall your
valley of grief. Walk softly and hear His footfalls.
He is here with us.*

CHAPTER 6

BEHOLDING GLORY

January 20, 1974

It snowed and then rained making a hard crust on top. The children were delighted. I dressed James and Elizabeth, layer upon layer (why are kids' boots so hard to get on?), and they went outside kicking up their heels, falling, giggling. Michael begged to go out too and I tried to dissuade him. It wasn't possible. So I reasoned he might as well learn what danger and misery are firsthand.

More layers and he puffed out the door. In a few minutes I heard him crying. Elizabeth was leading him to the house. He had slid down the icy hill until a tree stopped him. How did you get him, Elizabeth?

"I just crunched down to him and took his hand and he walked back in my crunches."

And since then I've thought of all the times Jesus has had to come after me when I was stuck, how He would crunch through the doubt or disillusionment or indifference, take my hand, and I'd walk back in His crunches, back to faith and peace of mind.

January 29, 1974

January is usually a long tiresome month, but this year I've had more satisfaction in small things. I spent some time sewing what seemed like dozens of tiny doll clothes out of scraps of material. James and Elizabeth, who play mommy and daddy to their dolls, were delighted with new outfits. I also made Elizabeth a little dress to match one of mine. We'll have a mother-daughter combination for spring.

The usual birthday glory.

And for Aunt Florabelle, another kind of glory. After a long siege of fighting a losing battle, she died and I took the children to the viewing. I've had this notion that one is never too young to learn of death. They went, cheering up the funeral home in the process, and came home with long thoughts. We read the story of the caterpillar as a cocoon, then becoming a beautiful butterfly. I told them that is like going to heaven. We leave a shell behind and fly away with Jesus.

Faith.

February 8, 1974

I seem to have midwinter doldrums. I'm trying to write but it's uphill all the way. *Decision* did accept a short article I wrote in December, about Jesus' return which has seemed real—and wonderful—for the first time in my life.

Plans to go to Beirut and the British Isles seem to be progressing slowly. It'll be so hard to leave my family. Ed isn't interested in going on the trip. He'll head for Missouri later, so I've been trying to get Marie Mc Conaghay to go with me. She needs a break if anyone does.

February 23, 1974

My little girl went to heaven early today.

Yesterday morning it was raining and unseasonably warm. Elizabeth said she had a sore throat, but ate a hearty dinner and played as usual. Ed took all three for a ride to buy balloons; then the sun shone brilliantly. The children and I scampered outside for a walk, but I noticed Elizabeth seemed tired. Everyone has had flu in the neighborhood and I reckoned it was now our turn. I told her to lie down awhile, but she soon got up and busily carried water outside to make mudpies with sidelong glances at me to see if I disapproved. I'm glad I didn't.

By evening she was very tired but played with Debbie, a neighbor-friend, before we hurried through the bath routine. Plucky as always, she washed her hair herself and I rinsed it. Beautiful soft golden stuff it was. My parents with a friend dropped in and the children glowed in their post-bath cleanliness, Elizabeth in a little pink nightgown that Cherry had made for her. We had lady-bugs on our windowsills and she shyly carried one to Dad's visitor.

Too tired to pray, she dropped off to sleep before I had James tucked in. I looked at her as I did every night and wondered how I had been given such a lovely little daughter.

At ten she awoke with fever, crying hard. She so seldom cried with illness that I was concerned and rocked her, murmuring endearments. Strangely, I wondered if I'd be with her later in life to see her married and bearing her children. One has so much suffering along the way. Would I be with her in it?

The fever declined some, but she clung to me when I tried to put her back in bed and so for the first—and last—time in her life, she went to bed with me. I asked if orange juice sounded good to her. "It sounds good to have you sit by me."

For two or three hours she half slept and tossed restlessly, but couldn't tell me what hurt. I still thought it was a rather miserable case of the flu and we would just try to make it through till morning as best we could. About 1:30 she began to throw up, heaving until I knew we had to do something to stop her. "I-wish-I-could-sleep," she said. And went limp as I picked her up.

Nearly frantic, I phoned for an ambulance while Ed with great presence of mind gave her mouth-to-mouth aid. He told me between breaths that this would keep her alive till help came and with her iron constitution she would be all right. But I feared, how I feared brain damage. She was so blue and unresponsive.

The Intensive Care Unit from St. Joseph's finally arrived and worked a couple more hours, but there was no response at all, just a faint pulse, then it disappeared. They took her to the hospital where she was pronounced dead.

Dead? Our healthiest child? I felt weak and lay down awhile at the hospital, but simply couldn't comprehend that the dearest, most enchanting little girl I ever knew was gone.

And I still can't. People have come all day, hundreds are praying for us, and I'm still numb. I know bleak loneliness will reach me later. For now, God has given strength to cope with visitors and our little boys. When we returned from the hospital, I was able to sit with

120

James and tell him calmly that our little sister was in heaven. We had lost her, but God was good to let us have her four years. He understood.

There was an autopsy this morning and I kept thinking I can't let them cut her. Maybe there's a mistake and she's still alive—but not if they cut her. How irrational the heart is.

The report said it was a massive viral infection that went inexplicably to her brain, probably the same flu bug that everyone else had, but affecting her in this way.

People are so kind. And how sad that only in times like this do we realize it.

February 24, 1974

Today we saw her, Ed and I, in her red and white Sunday school outfit. I sat awhile with her and remembered what a rare treasure she has been these four years. Her little hands that were so warm and competent, now still, had traces of magic marker on them that wouldn't scrub off.

Elizabeth had health, wit, beauty, intelligence, in a sense the most "perfect" gift I ever had. It struck me that God gave His perfect Son as a sacrifice, and what that has done for humanity. But at what a price.

Dare I pray that our girl will in some way reach out and point others to that greater Gift? That would give meaning even to this.

February 26, 1974

Snow has made the world white and pure. It somehow fits. James said, "Jesus is teaching Elizabeth how to make snow 'cause she knows I like it."

Two neighbors, Dave McNary and Jerry Weldy, flew in from Missouri. Old friends of Ed's, they warmed his heart and gave him a sense of home folks. At the service this afternoon we sang "Amazing Grace," our family hymn, with Michael's voice chiming above everyone else—"When we've been there ten thousand years/ Bright shining as the sun." The song has run full course now. One of us is brighter, more shining than she has ever been before. I was able to sing, to *sing* all four stanzas this afternoon.

I can't seem to think of food, but our Twin Valley Chapel women helped, bringing us meals and providing supper for a huge crowd after the funeral. It has comforted me to think that people have cared and helped so much, many anonymously.

The hardest part was leaving her at the cemetery. To think that one so warm and vibrant is lying in the earth, that I can never put her to bed again, or comb her hair, or hear her laugh.

Yet the other side of the picture is in my memory verse assignment this week. When I toss in bed, I say it over and over and it helps me sleep, one verse especially. "Father, I will that they also, whom thou hast given me, *be with me where I am;* that they may *behold thy glory.* . . ." Elizabeth is beholding His glory and surely a little of it will spill over to us.

March 10, 1974

What would we do without our little boys? James says, "The days are getting happier." I'm glad they are. He's had a big burden for such small shoulders.

For me they are worse. Every room is crowded with

memories and I keep coming across her little treasures tucked here and there. There's such a heaviness and disinterest in life that accompanies sorrows. I went back to school Friday thinking that would help and I seemed to see a little blond ghost follow me all day. "Surely he hath borne our griefs, and carried our sorrow." I say that over and over, but it's in faith. I don't *feel* it. My emotions are in pieces inwardly, yet God has helped me more than I can say in being able just to control myself, to meet each day's routine and obligation, to smile.

A huge moon these nights. Crocuses and tulips coming, some that she helped to plant last fall. Spring. And I can think only of that grave, that beautiful little face sagging, crumbling. O Death, there *is* a sting.

How many times I held her and told her that I loved her, that she was my only little girl.

"Take now thy son, thine only son . . . whom thou lovest. . . ." Abraham was spared. I wasn't.

God wasn't either.

March 14, 1974

People note my composure, my faith, my smile. If they knew how often faith lies shattered around me in pieces and I can only gather up the bits and ask God to make a new thing out of it. Such blackness and fear at times. I know now why Paul said, "If in this life only we have hope in Christ, we are of all men most miserable." So utterly miserable I am much of the time these days. What if, *what if* I never see her again?

The boys and I have had versions of the flu these weeks and that doesn't help. Michael goes around saying, "Me don't know what to do." Elizabeth was his constant playmate and he's lonesome now. James is lost too. "Mommy, I can hardly believe Elizabeth died. I have to think she's better off. Then I can stop thinking about her." He found some little colored scraps of paper she had made and given to him. With tears he showed me and stowed them away in his box that he calls his office.

The death of one's child is like an amputation. Something is missing and one is always conscious of the lack. There is this sense of physical pain, as though I'd been struck a heavy blow. "My soul refused to be comforted. I remembered God, and was troubled. . . . Will the Lord cast off for ever? . . . Hath God forgotten to be gracious? . . . And I said, This is my infirmity: but I will remember the years of the right hand of the most High. I will remember the works of the Lord . . . I will meditate also of all thy work, and talk of thy doings."

I will.

March 23, 1974

A month since our girl left us. The shock is gone now and I see her everywhere—and nowhere. Sunday we went to see Jonas and Lydia Smoker, an Amish couple who lost their four-year-old girl just a month before ours. They had written us a sweet letter, and Lydia's face is just as sweet as the letter. We've had mail every day and people have prayed and been in touch, especially our friends at church.

Ed has been quietly strong these days. Not a demonstrative man, he has phoned folks and tended to matters that need to be done. He says little, but I have appreciated his stability.

Marie and I are flying to Beirut in April unless something turns up to prevent either of us. Friends have encouraged me to go and it probably is wise to get my thoughts elsewhere. Marie will likely have some crisis come up with her family to prevent her going, but maybe not, maybe not. God knows she needs a change.

Mom and Dad are paying for our transportation. They are thoroughly generous as always, and we'll be staying with friends and relatives all along the way, making our costs much less and the benefits greater. The diversion and change should help us both, but it has been an effort to force myself to make the arrangements.

"Lay up for yourselves treasures in heaven." I have, Lord; I have now.

April 5, 1974

Tonight constant thoughts have intruded as I study for Bible club tomorrow. Facing *that* these Saturday mornings has probably been one of the hardest struggles each week. How she sang, her clear rich voice ringing out, "Rejoice, rejoice, and again I say rejoice."

Yet I think the worst is over. My appetite is slowly returning after having to force myself to eat. I would not want to relive these last six weeks. They were grim ones indeed.

Mrs. McLeod, Alice's mother, wrote me from Wisconsin the other day that she had got up at 3:00 a.m. to pray for us that morning. Did she remember the pit one goes through after the initial shock? She, of all people, knows how to pray and it was about that time that light and warmth seemed to get inside me again. God answered her prayer, not in a spectacular miracle, but in a consciousness of despair and heaviness beginning to lift, of doubt disappearing.

It is Jesus coming to me as He has countless times through the years, taking my hand, and I'm starting to walk in His crunches again.

April 14, 1976 (Easter Sunday)

Friends. People whom I haven't seen since 1966, but the years fall away as we meet again. We're staying with Les and Agnes de Smidt this week in Beirut, but over Easter weekend we've come outside the city to Kfarchima and are soaking up beauty and hospitality with Hazel St. John, my principal when I lived here. This morning she gave me an Easter card she'd made with the words inside, "Because He lives, you (and yours) shall live also."

Here in this part of the world is where it all happened. Jesus, the Son of God, came to earth, died, and rose again. For us. For me. If He hadn't, I might as well quit now and jump over the balcony to the courtyard beneath. There are no other alternatives. It is life—or death. I have never seen it so clearly before.

Beirut is the same chaotically beautiful city. The traffic is worse, if that's possible, and has given Marie some bad moments. We wandered through the market the other day, hovered in the gold souk, but walked on. Inflation is here too.

April 16, 1974

Les took us to Baalbek and I am always aghast at the immensity of that place. On the way home we climbed up, up above the Litani Dam, over the top, and down to the Maasar Cedars where we had tea under the spacious, spreading branches.

Tonight I gave Douglas Anderson as head of the Lebanon Evangelical Mission a check, the money from Elizabeth's memorial fund. He told me it will be used in the translation and publication of one of Kenneth Taylor's books for children.

Who knows? Elizabeth may touch more little girls and boys through her death than she ever could have in life.

April 18, 1974

We're in London with Rosalind who is looking bonny as she awaits the birth of her second child. Today she took us to John Wesley's home where I played the organ of his brother Charles. Some tourists were in the room, good Methodists from Maryland, and we sang some of his hymns together. One of those lovely moments that are little preludes of future harmony and love.

Across the street was an old cemetery. There we ate our lunch near the grave of John Bunyan. The communion of saints, past and present

April 28, 1974

Ireland is a little emerald gem in the sea. It is heartbreaking to see barbed wire, British soldiers, tanks, and fear in the North.

We flew across from Scotland after a short visit with Mary Rogers Smith, another friend from Beirut days. Her small twin daughter was uncannily like Elizabeth a couple years ago.

Now we're at Aunt Annie's in this little Donegal town of Creeslough and we seem to spend a lot of time by her cozy peat fire sipping tea. I've visited most of the clan who have welcomed us warmly.

It hasn't even rained.

What a gift this trip has been, sharing with friends, getting my mind and heart stretched and away from myself, visiting with Marie along the way and knowing she is the one who has the heaviest burden.

May 7, 1974

A grand arrival at Philadelphia last Thursday, but only two little faces waiting. The third one so very absent. But how good to have these dear little boys. How desolate our home would be without them.

I've had some tired, lonely days since then, but seem to be recovering slowly. Yesterday I went to school but coming home again always emphasizes the emptiness.

The question Job asked: what *is* the meaning of suffering, not just mine but the whole world's? How are my views too small, too narrow? God is so big. What is heaven *really* like? It's got to be good if it can make up for all the miseries, tragedies, dullness, and disappointments of earth. How do I make faith real and alive to Jane tonight at Bible study?

May 12, 1974

Gradually peace, like our garden, is growing. I planted some flowers on the grave and managed quite well. The boys were along and we walked around and read headstones of several loved ones, including a tiny one of Miles Russell who died at fifteen months. My little grandmother once stood there and wept and wondered why. She knows now.

From Oswald Chambers' *My Utmost for His Highest:* "A saint's life is in the hands of God like a bow and arrow in the hands of an archer. God is aiming at something the saint cannot see, and He stretches and strains, and every now and again the saint says—'I cannot stand any more.' God does not heed, He goes on stretching till His purpose is in sight, then He lets fly. Trust yourself in God's hands."

May 29, 1974

Ed has been in Missouri a couple weeks and we are managing fine except at night. I miss him when I wake up and the bed is empty. Somehow I keep going over that last night with Elizabeth when she slept with me. With Ed here it doesn't haunt me as much.

Both boys have been sick. James had the mumps, and in the middle of the night that is worrisome too. I never used to worry much about their childish ailments.

We do lots of visiting and entertaining by day and grub in our garden frequently. Whatever would we do in life without work? And people? Russ, Peg, and their girls took us to the zoo on Sylvia's birthday. A fun day but poignant too as James and I recalled how many times we'd planned such a trip with Elizabeth. We all roared into Uncle Bob's afterward and had cake and Aunt Margaret's "tea" which, simply put, is an abundant supper.

Grandma Read is in good health, mentally and physically, according to Ed, and I still feel sad that we haven't been able to take care of her these years. She is ninety-two, a remarkable age.

Gradually a dream, a hope is building up, one that I've had since I read *Little Men* as a child, that we can adopt a little girl. Ed used to say we would do well to raise our own but, dear man, he sounds interested now. Hubby is good to me.

June 18, 1974

"Lord, to whom shall we go? thou hast the words of eternal life. And we believe and are sure that thou art that Christ, the Son of the living God."

Lord, Elizabeth must be with You. There is no one else. I love You more than ever now. I've wondered lately, whom do I want to see first, You or her. And the answer came so easily. All down through the years You've been with me and kept me alive, the real me, and fulfilled every vague longing and given meaning when there was none and joy in the morning after nights of weeping.

I *want* to see You, Lord Jesus. Strange, I'm weeping now. You know all the loneliness and longing and love I feel—and maybe You're weeping with me. Acquainted with grief You are, but You're also the One who gave the woman a well of life, of pure joy springing up in her heart.

Spring thou up within my heart,
Rise to all eternity.

June 27, 1974

These have been some of Michael's meditations lately.

"Our cat died. Our Ewizabef died. Same thing."

"Them are my thwends." (Grammie and Angie.)

Prayer at bedtime: *"Dear Jesus, help me be good. I wuv you. Pray for Ewizabef up a heaven. She happy and singing. Pray Jesus taking care of she. Amen"*

July 7, 1974

Today we had communion at church and I was conscious of the suffering of Christ, His loneliness and the drops of blood in Gethsemane, the agony of the cross.

I remembered something from Elizabeth's last day. In their play she had scratched Michael's face so that it bled a little. He cried and I comforted him.

A couple hours later, as though she were straightening all her little matters, she went to him and put her arm around him and said quietly, "Michael, I'm sorry I made you bleed." She did it herself with no prompting from me.

This morning it came back to me and I prayed, "Lord Jesus, I'm sorry I made You bleed."

July 19, 1974

The summer that I had dreaded in the wee hours of the morning is moving along and I'm busier than I thought possible. That is good, what I prayed for in fact.

I'm having five-day clubs in several neighborhoods near here. I visit folks, invite their children to someone's lawn each day at 10:30 a.m., and we have a Good News Club for about forty-five minutes. This last week has been in such a poor community. One little crippled boy with a beautiful smile literally drags himself out each morning. Several are retarded as well. One is pregnant. I keep wondering if I even begin to reach them, but then love is a universal language.

And our dear friend, Violet Lewis, from Missouri is planning to fly here in August. She lost a 14-month-old daughter years ago and so we have more to share than ever. That will fill up a couple weeks.

All along I've been doing lots of canning and freezing. It's a profitable thing to do with today's prices. We had a bumper crop of strawberries.

Perhaps the most remarkable occupation of this summer has been gathering together material written in my diary, in notebooks, and bits of paper, much of it on the run, gathering, sorting, editing, and finally putting it together as a book. Me, writing a book. It has been a kind of therapy going over these years, seeing how God has led, reliving all the sweet moments with our children, and being glad that I had a daughter for four years.

Looking back, there have been many ups and downs, unexpected hopes, shattered dreams, such a lot of laughter and joy, some sadness, and this year our great tragedy, yet through every bit of it is God. "All the way my Savior leads me," says Fanny Crosby. She's right.

August 3, 1974

Yesterday we finally got the stone on Elizabeth's grave and it was the wrong color, gray instead of rose. I was upset and felt weepy all day, yet I know it's not really important. Such a poor thing a stone is to remember a living, little girl, her winsome smile, her sweetness, all the blend of femininity and laughter and breath-catching beauty.

Psalm 116 tonight, an old friend. "For thou hast delivered my soul from death, mine eyes from tears, and my feet from falling. I will walk before the Lord in the land of the living." He is the God of the living, not the dead—and Elizabeth is more alive now than she ever was with us. He is her God and mine.

A brief reply from the adoption agency that we

queried. When a child is available and they can do the home study, we'll be notified. In the meantime there will be meetings, study groups, and the like.

An adopted daughter. Could this be my "land of the living"? All my life I've wanted a girl, a daughter to share with, to give to her some of what has been given so freely to me. I would give, but how much more she would give to me. It's that great paradox of life that the more we give the more we receive.

August 23, 1974
Dear little girl,

It's six months since you've gone.

All day I've seen you out of the corner of my eye. Running as hard as you could through the lawn while I cut the grass. I always loved the back view of you. There was something so jauntily feminine about the way you ran. . . .

And I saw you helping Michael whenever he cried. You would put your arm around him, kiss the hurt, and lead him to me. He misses you a lot. . . .

When I went shopping for groceries, you were there, just a couple steps behind me, laughing and talking with James, onlookers noticing your loveliness, and my mixture of pride and concern lest you become conceited. . . .

I saw you on the swing at Grammie and Grampie's, wanting to go higher, your hair blowing in the wind. . . .

At the dinner table I watched you, eyes huge as you gazed out the window and looked at trees blowing or a helicopter go by; then they twinkled into a laugh at something you said or thought of. . . .

Can you possibly know how much we miss you? Do

you ever think of us? Or are you so changed, so complete, so full of love and beauty that we are forgotten? Are you still a little girl or did you become a woman, mature, wise, perfect? Somehow I think God wanted a child, a daughter, and you're still just four years old. But eternal life must mean eternal growth. When I see you, you will be changed, you will have grown. Yet who knows? In the now of eternity maybe I can travel backward and see all the girl-years we missed and make them up.

It is beyond me. Too much speculation makes my head reel. Who can comprehend heaven? At times it's all I can do to believe in it.

The heart, though, knows its own sorrow and joy. These last months have been outlined by memories, some that stab and make me anguished, others that warm and comfort, some that make me laugh. You were so unexpectedly funny at times.

I found your little apron one day when housecleaning and thought of all the times you helped me. The last photos we have are of you and Michael washing dishes, your hair long and curling down your back, and one of my aprons reaching to your ankles.

I shall never enter Good's store without thinking of the last time you were there. You begged for a little ninety-nine-cent handbag which I stoically refused, telling you that for spring you could have a new pink outfit and a white handbag. For once I had decided to indulge my love and dress you in something extra pretty instead of Good's irregulars. Now you are clothed in purity and light and a plastic handbag is laughable. Why do I cry?

Your last birthday party in January—you remember how your friends couldn't come because of illness? And you said quietly, "Next year, Mommy, lots of people will come." I wonder, are there birthdays in heaven?

One night I dreamed about you and heard you laugh. It was so clear and hearty, and then it faded, faded. I reach in vain to hear it again.

Ah, little one, your mother is weak and weeping. I miss you a thousand times a day. Sometimes when I drift off to sleep, in a split second the loss of you overwhelms me and I wake up trembling.

Yet there are times, not often, but times when I sense joy not in spite of but *because* you are in heaven. These are glimpses into eternity, however fleeting, that give meaning even to what seem the senseless things of life and assurance that someday we will understand completely.

"You have everything when you have Christ." He is yours, Elizabeth, and you will never know a single lack or shed a tear or feel terror or disappointment or pain. You have found your niche (Jesus called them mansions) and it is yours forever. You are far beyond me and my imaginings, you've missed so much that is bad and gained all that is good. I cannot wish you back.

What more can I say? I believe in Jesus, that He is with you. And with me. That all things *do* work together for good to them that love God. Part of me is with you, I feel empty, but someday I'll be full and complete, more *whole* than I've ever been before.

Until then, I walk by faith.

Lovingly,
Mommy

"SURELY GOODNESS AND MERCY
SHALL FOLLOW ME ALL THE DAYS
OF MY LIFE"

Into a new phase of life God led us as a family, and we were astounded at the goodness and mercy shown to us. He answered a multitude of prayers and enriched us—forever.

CHAPTER 7

JOY COMES IN THE MORNING

September 20, 1974

Last night I went to a meeting in Lancaster for adoptive parents-to-be. Sponsored by PACO (Parents of Adopted Children Organization), it was mostly a panel discussion by parents. One family had "eight children at last count." The head of our agency has twelve, three "home-made," nine adopted. I left, feeling we should take half a dozen at least. This has been a burden and dream of mine for years, since childhood in fact, so that I can hardly believe it may finally be realized.

It amazes me that Ed has not squelched the idea before this. As a whim of mine he is willing to consider it, but it's quite another thing to go forward with it, pay the fees, fill out endless forms, and actually take a specific tangible child.

We shall see. If God wills it, she'll come.

September 24, 1974

My dear little elder son. Last week he wondered if God

minded if you liked your mommy better than Him. I remember pondering that.

He is getting along better in kindergarten. His teacher seemed to be such a grump, and I was afraid he'd turn off school entirely. As a class mother, I've become better acquainted with her and have realized again that one should never be critical of another till you've walked a mile in his moccasins. Mrs. Jennings is divorced and holding two jobs to put her daughters through college. Each day after school she works at the shopping center. She must be exhausted. I told James and it helps him to understand and pray for her. He thinks it's dreadful that she has no daddy.

Michael is wheezing, coughing, awake so much at night with this allergy of his. Nights are long and frightening with a sick boy.

At Bible study last week we considered John 4, a favorite of mine. The woman at the well received not just a drink but a whole well of water to take with her. Jane was here, intrigued and maybe a little thirsty. I recall Oswald Chambers' statement, "You cannot give someone what you've got, but you can make him homesick for what you have." I wonder, is she homesick?

October 23, 1974

I just listened to the last part of the *Messiah* on the radio and was moved to tears at the grandeur and glory of those matchless words, "I know that my Redeemer liveth, and . . . in my *flesh* I shall see God." I, sinful, fallen flesh shall one day be adorned with light and holiness and look on God Himself.

Our girl will too.

November 18, 1974

Today we sent in our application for a little Korean girl. I am so excited. It included photos, an initial payment, a statement of faith (Holt is a distinctly Christian agency), a copy of our last income tax return, and the application form itself. My dear hubby signed it though I know he isn't so wildly enthusiastic as I am. Ed loves me and God is hearing my prayers, a combination that is powerful.

We thought of a Vietnamese child, but the government there is strict. Very few children are allowed to leave. I can't bear to wait years.

December 6, 1974

Today we decorated our Christmas tree, one that Dad gave us from his place. James was beside himself with delight, Michael thrilled but more quietly. It looks beautiful and I managed fine till I came across the little snowman of Elizabeth's—and she wasn't here to put it on. I ached all evening.

To think she's in heaven, where it all started. Our tinsel and lights and candles are paltry beside that glory.

"I am the living bread which came from heaven: if any man eat of this bread, he shall live for ever."

December 31, 1974

Great heaviness tonight. Ed was at work and I couldn't even manage to get to the New Year's Eve service. It just seemed too much effort. And I bawled when I read the boys their stories, something I've not done often, thank God.

Perhaps it's because as the year ends, I'm moving

away so rapidly from Elizabeth and her brief life on earth. It seems to be spinning backward into memories that will inevitably get wispier. And yet, and yet, the opposite *must* be true, that I'm getting closer to her each hour, each day. As Spurgeon says, this year may be the one when He will come.

January 24, 1975

A multitude of indignities today from six classes of tenth grade. I felt a little frayed and decided, as I often do, that substitutes are certainly not overpaid.

This is the eve of our little girl's birthday, the time when I would bake and decorate a cake and she would have loved to help. Perhaps she'll have a celebration anyway and sit on Jesus' lap and welcome all the children and angels to her party. Even heaven must be adorned by her smile.

We are having the Tuckeys here for supper tomorrow to help us over the hump. It has been a hard week.

And yet, there are lifts along the way, two beautiful letters—one from Agnes in Beirut, the other from Betty Ann—to tell me I'm thought of these days. Friends are good.

And at last, a letter from Holt to tell us a home study will be done on us. For that we'll use the York Agency that impressed me so much, Tressler-Lutheran Service Associates. I still hold my breath when I think of another daughter.

I wonder where she is now.

February 24, 1975

This has been a winter of illness for us. We have all

had the flu, but Saturday night, the anniversary of Elizabeth's death, was the worst. Michael became delirious and I thought it just couldn't be. Aspirin and cold cloths brought the fever down. Twice it happened, and I took him to bed with me and lived with memories all night.

Yet there was a strange peace and poise all weekend and I found out why at church. So many said they were praying for us. They prayed so faithfully last year also and it helped immeasurably.

Ed has been quite ill too which added to the general misery. We invited Don and Marilyn Barto for dinner Sunday to keep us occupied, and even though I'd been awake most of the night with Michael, it was good for me to have the responsibility and distraction of guests. Marilyn lost twins a few months ago.

It was a weekend of afflictions. My latest manuscript was returned with valid criticsim. It's hard to accept, like criticism of one's children, even though probably true. I must revise *again*.

"The Lord is good, a stronghold in the day of trouble; and he knoweth them that trust in him."

March 6, 1975

I just read a most amazing book, *Mourning Song*, by Joyce Landorf, which so adequately describes the stages of grief and how to cope with them. I wish I'd had it a year ago. I must list them lest I forget.

1. Denial (I can't let them do an autopsy—they'll kill her).
2. Resentment (Lord, why pick on me? Why *my* little girl, prettier and sweeter than any other).
3. Plea bargaining (Well, Lord, You took of my best; now

answer some of my prayers. Don't I deserve that at least?).

4. Depression (When the waves of grief rolled over me and I doubted heaven and love and God Himself).
5. Creative acceptance (Is this the adoption of a daughter, not to replace Elizabeth, but to help us accept her loss and share our love with another who will fill her own place in our home?).

There is progress and lots of regression in grief, one goes through each stage many times, but I think I have passed a turning point since Elizabeth is gone a year. I used to think, last year at this time she was with me and we did this and this together. Now I seem to be relieved of the constant reminiscing. There are sharp flashbacks to be sure, but not a constant drain.

And I think so often of our little Korean girl, wondering where she is now and the loneliness and hurts she may have. I pray for her each day.

March 19, 1975

We had our first adoption meeting in York on Monday night. Ed will go to just three out of the nine because of work. On the way I stopped at our little grave and thought of our two girls and how God does things, that we would not be reaching out to this unknown child if we still had Elizabeth.

The meetings are held at Barbara Tremitiere's house, mother of thirteen. She's an unusual woman and I left feeling like we ought to apply for three or four children at least.

Our boys are getting excited about the prospect of a sister, James especially. Michael is a little young to understand what it means, and also placid by nature, so like Elizabeth. One night James, full of questions, wondered where these children come from. I told him some parents can't keep or don't want their children. Other parents are dead and the children are orphans. "That's better, Mommy, than not wanting them," he said.

March 29, 1975

This morning when I woke, Elizabeth seemed to hover near. Strange, how one has a sense of especially missing a person, longing to have just a glimpse, to hear one word. I wonder, *was* she near me? James felt it too and said he wished he could take just that little tractor and truck to heaven with him. Why? Because Elizabeth liked them so. I remembered they played together often with them.

In the mail was—at last—an acceptance from *Moody Monthly* of the article I wrote about our girl last summer. Along with that from Beirut were three copies of the book that her memorial fund printed in Arabic, *Devotions for Children* by Kenneth Taylor. Was Elizabeth here to see the mail? After that I did not have the overwhelming sense of her.

Tomorrow is Easter. "The Lord is risen indeed."

April 9, 1975

Since Elizabeth's death, James has had a strong sense of mortality. He was especially concerned about Michael this last winter when he was so ill. (He sensed our fear too even though we tried to hide it.) Would Michael go to heaven if he died? "Mommy, you should pray with him to accept Jesus."

I explained that Michael is young and really didn't seem to understand what it meant. This didn't satisfy.

This morning James just beaming, with Mike in tow, came downstairs and told me that now Michael has Jesus in his heart too. "I prayed and told him to pray after me. He *did*, Mommy."

His brother's keeper indeed.

April 18, 1975

We're planning to go to Missouri in May for a visit, our first as a family since we left. Violet Lewis has invited us to stay at her home, a kind gesture on her part. It will be a difficult trip, two days of constant driving each way, and an emotional thing for me to see our home again.

At the adoption meeting on Monday, Barb implied we may get one of the Vietnamese children who have been suddenly airlifted from Saigon these last weeks. I can't believe that is possible, or I should say, I am afraid to believe and get my hopes up. People have waited years for Vietnamese children. The fact that we want an older child rather than a baby is a help though.

And the fact that we have filled out the papers and are still in the running is a miracle. From my earnings this last winter we have been able to save a sizable amount to cover the costs. Thank you, Lord.

April 25, 1975

Tonight at 11:00 p.m. the phone rang with Barb of Tressler-Lutheran on the other end. She has a little Vietnamese girl, age five, for us—*tomorrow*. I ran downstairs to greet Ed as he came home from work, laughing and crying. God *does* answer prayer. I'm too excited to sleep and came to write in here and to thank Him for this remarkable event. I want to phone everyone but it's too late.

A name . . . Susan I've always loved, and perhaps Joy to express what she's bringing us . . . I've wondered so much about this new little girl, her parents, what heartache she's had, what loneliness and fear . . . and memories of Elizabeth are all mingled with anticipation and I'm one big emotional blob. . . . This morning as I often do, I went through her clothes—I get hungry to see them—and thought again of His pathways, how difficult they are, how surprising, but how unspeakably dear He has been and is.

April 26, 1975

Very little sleep through the night and I scampered out of bed at 6:00 a.m. and across the road to tell the folks. Dad was eating breakfast and he choked up when I told him, then called Mom to hear the news. They have been hoping and praying with us.

Back to my own youngsters who were waking up. James positively glowed and even Michael was excited.

Then on to more prosaic matters such as celebrating Michael's fourth birthday. We always save the party for the weekend nearest the actual date. I burned the cake in my preoccupied joy as I listened again to the lovely song "Surely Goodness and Mercy" sung on a record by Bev Shea and the London Crusade Choir. How long ago it has been since I first heard it in London and what a lot has happened since. How enriched my life has been, all because of His mercy and goodness.

Jane and her kids came for the birthday party. Michael

was much more composed than I. As I exploded to Jane about our news, she remarked rather wistfully, "Maybe God does answer prayer."

It was beautiful to shop for little girl's clothes again. I got basics, except a pink frilly dress for Sunday school, this on our way to York where we were to meet her. Ed and the boys were along, all of us a potpourri of excitement, fear, joy, and some aching memories.

The receiving families waited in a room at Tressler headquarters, some of them old-timers at adoption, others novices like ourselves. Suddenly the word went around the room, "They're coming." A van was bringing the children from the Baltimore Airport where they had flown from Fort Benning, Georgia.

It was a moving experience to see the children walk in one by one, or be carried in. There were a few babies, many children, a few teens, a boy on crutches, each one coming to *parents* for the first time. A dear little girl was handed to me and we sat and cried together.

She is adorable. We got our first smile at McDonald's when she saw food. Clutching a doll all the way home, she finally laid it down as soon as she arrived here, covered it, and proceeded to make herself at home. Such a competent little soul she is.

Ed fell in love with her immediately. I'm so glad.

April 27, 1975

My wits all lost or disarranged, I was glad I'd made chicken corn soup yesterday to heat for dinner. Susan ate four bowls of it and did the dishes afterward—perfectly. She wants so much to please. As I snapped a photo of her, I recalled the last picture I have of Elizabeth is of her and

Michael washing dishes together.

Company of all kinds this afternoon, not the best thing for a child who has so many adjustments to make, but she seems to take it in stride. Her physical, mental, and emotional health are remarkably sturdy, all answers to prayer.

Ed told me that Susan cut the doll's hair today. Did he try to stop her? No, he said rather sheepishly, he helped her. Dear funny family.

May 16, 1975

Since our plans were to go to Missouri, we carried through even though Susan had been with us just a week. She seems secure as long as we're with her. It was no mean task to get three children through two long days of driving, especially when one of them did not speak English, cried off and on from sheer frustration and homesickness, and none of them took a nap. Yawn.

Now we are here staying in Violet's house, a tight fit, but adequate and comfortable. I'm nervous about the house. The other day a heavy plate tumbled off the china cupboard, hitting both Susan and Michael. Mike's head bled, and Susan has a knot. Fortunately the plate is whole.

It seems strange to see our lovely home and not live in it, to remember my children's baby days in it, to see Grandma Read again and recall the frustration and failure with her.

Grandma is in an excellent home with good care and seems happy, as happy as one can be in bed all the time. Ninety-three now, a great age. I'm glad the boys could see her again. For James, she was just a a faint memory and Michael hadn't seen her since he was seven months. Now they all three know her.

May 29, 1975

One of the things for which I thank God daily is a husband who could open his heart and life to a little orphan and accept her as his own. Many men couldn't or wouldn't. It is relatively easy to love one's own flesh and blood, quite another to accept and love a stranger of another nationality and race and culture. (But then isn't that what God does—accepts aliens, strangers, and far-off ones?)

It's lovely to see Ed with Susan. They communicate in spite of language barriers, singing, laughing, teasing. With true feminine instinct she can manage him already.

All the shadows of doubt, how would she fit in, could we love her enough, would she be accepted in our home, our church, our community, all have fled in the sunshine of this tangible little person.

June 10, 1975

Today was the last day of school. Susan has fit in well, crying occasionally, but mostly going obediently with James. And he has been so proud to take "my sister" with him. After school she runs in, bursting to tell me what happened yet so limited with her English. With her body language and James' interpretation, we can usually figure it out.

She ran into a little Vietnamese girl at school, from the same orphanage. I can imagine the pure delight to see a friendly face and hear a familiar tongue.

She told us one day about her airplane trips, how she

cried, got sick, bumped her head, all graphically demonstrated. A little ham she is. I'm so glad God gave me *interesting* children.

How dear they are, all four of them.

June 15, 1975 (Given to Ed with love on Father's Day)
Why I love my hubby–
1. He's a superb babysitter and practices it frequently.
2. He has room in his heart for an adopted child.
3. He empties the garbage and burns paper.
4. He does dishes when he wouldn't have to.
5. He has a nice smile.
6. He can fix things.
7. He eats anything I feed him—without grumbling.
8. He makes love just right for me.
9. He likes me.

June 18, 1975

As time goes on, we get little bits of information about Susan's past. From An Lac Orphanage in Saigon, she lived there all her life up to now. Madame Ngai, a remarkable woman originally from Hanoi, was the founder of the orphanage in 1954 and has mothered thousands of children ever since. Many of them were left in little baskets outside the gate at night, to be gathered in in the morning. Our daughter was one of these abandoned waifs.

Is her mother alive? Does she ever ache to see her? Or has she forgotten? Was she a woman of the streets, a communist perhaps, or just a destitute peasant woman who could not feed another mouth and thought it a kindness to give up her daughter to a better home than she could provide? I pray for her if she is yet alive. She has such an exquisite little girl.

July 2, 1975

We made July 1 her birthday, certainly a handy thing to be able to choose a time that fits into one's calendar of Important Family Events. She received her first birthday gifts from Aunt Sadie and Aunt Ruth yesterday, her face glowing, and she's been talking about them ever since. They're now tucked away in her shoe box of valuables.

There have been humps, adjustments, times when I've been totally nonplussed to know just how to handle a child who speaks so little English, who is new to us, the behavior we expect, the food we eat, the terms of discipline (and she *is* mischievous)—yet at no time have I wondered why we got her. She is ours in a profound way and could never leave again.

I often look at her in bed at night and wonder if anyone ever hovered over her before, prayed for her, touched her, smoothed back her hair, did any of the motherly things that one takes so for granted in a natural family.

She prays now. Head bowed devoutly, hands folded, the dark brown eyes shut tightly. "Dear Lovey Da, Mommy, Daddy, Tsusan, Jem, Michael, Grandma, Amen."

September 10, 1975

After three years of being a battered substitute, I am now teaching full time. And in our Twin Valley Bible Academy which was whisked into being in the last three months. Pastor Palmer has a special heart for Christian

152

education and encouraged the school into being.

It is good to be with respectful students, to be appreciated by parents and other staff, to pray together as a faculty, and to take James and Susan with me each day. Perhaps it's too easy, too secluded from the needs of the world—I must make the effort to keep my avenues open to people—but for now, it is a balm, a restoration to my teaching ego.

Susan is blooming in the atmosphere of personal love and attention. She adores her teacher, Marilyn Barto, and is learning rapidly. Madame Ngai had ingrained a love for learning within her and Susan has yearned to read and write. No more tears going to school these days. In fact, she regrets Saturdays.

October 8, 1975

Today some records came from Gospel Recordings in Vietnamese. I had sent for them hoping to be able to keep Susan's language alive. It seems a real loss to forget it as rapidly as most children do.

She loved them and sang loudly as I cooked supper. After awhile I noticed she was quiet. I found her lying on the couch crying heartbrokenly.

For the first time she was homesick and said she wanted to go to Vietnam. I could not calm her, but knowing how hunger and tiredness upset her, I got the meal on the table. What I could not do, fried chicken did. She soon smiled, asked for seconds, then played all evening.

I shall have to be careful when I play them again.

February 11, 1976

A lovely surprise from Ed when I arrived home from

school. There was a potted azalea plant covered with buds ready to bloom into a bright red valentine. This past year or more God has washed away a lot of bitterness, tiredness, old resentments, and given us an increased love. We are rich indeed.

February 21, 1976

Some stunning news came from Beirut recently, more shocking (to me) even than the war. Leslie de Smidt was killed in a freakish accident. Trying to contain and suffocate a fire, he slipped off a balcony railing and fell to his death—with Agnes watching. Probably the most vibrantly alive man I've ever known. I wonder, has he seen our angel-girl yet? They would enjoy one another.

She will soon have spent two years in eternity. And what is that? It is as though she has *always* been there, as though this is what she was created for. I am still amazed that a part of me, a child of my womb, has seen and known God Himself.

April 11, 1976

How swiftly life goes, like a weaver's shuttle, as Job says. There are intimations of mortality everywhere. The news from Beirut continues to be heartbreaking with increased war and people fleeing, hunger and devastation everywhere. Many of the LEM folk are in Cyprus now.

And at Narvon we are engrossed in our own local cycles of life and spring. The children found a toad living under a corner of our house and sunning himself on warm days. It was their pet, they said, and there seemed to be a reciprocal feeling on his part. Poor thing, he must have ventured out on too chilly a day, for they found him stiff and cold. They had a burial for him and put flowers, wee periwinkle, on the grave. Susan said he'll "melt," then go to heaven. Perhaps he will.

The same evening our cat turned up with a new kitten.

May 9, 1976

Susan has been here a year now. Tonight she wondered if her skin would be white in heaven. I assured her she was a dear little brown girl and doubtless would be in heaven too, that Jesus liked her that way. She looked so relieved, then wished wistfully that I was brown too.

We talked awhile about that, how colors don't matter, how God made us and we are beautiful to Him, that I *loved* her and wouldn't have her look any other way. Then, would she like a brown sister?

Her eyes shone in the dark room. We decided to pray together for that—and for a bigger house to put us all in. We are spilling over in this present one.

Another daughter and a bigger house. Sounds audacious, impossible. "Before they call I will answer, and while they are yet speaking I will hear."

o   o   o

As I think of it, all prayer is audacious, a marvelous blend of humility and reaching for the stars. It is finding out the will of God and then asking him to accomplish it. I gasp often at the directness of His power, the sudden wrenches He gives, the strange and dark roads where He leads, the profound lessons He teaches. Yet I am drawn irresistibly to trust the compassion, the infinite detail that could only be the outworking of love Himself.

155

For example, I would not be married to Ed and the mother of our children if I had not gone to Beirut, much against my natural instincts, and spent three years there. All the detailed and exact planning that went into our meeting, Ed and I, after what seemed like years of aimless wandering. The crusade at Wembley Stadium during my stopover in London, the publication of the article in *Decision*, the year of waiting in Narvon were on God's calendar and our meeting was perfectly punctual.

Yet more sobering is this knowledge, that we would not be the parents of Susan if Elizabeth had not died. This astounds, confounds, *awes* me, that God gave us our first daughter to love a few years, and then took her, perhaps to adorn heaven, she was so beautiful. Meanwhile He had an orphanage in Saigon under His eye, and He was preserving a sparkling little Oriental girl to be one of ours—and one of His. The communist siege came to the city, the baby airlift was on, world events were fitting into His plan—to give one small "other" child to us.

I wonder why. What does He have in store for her? For us?

I can understand His ability to swing stars, to move nations, to end wars as befitting His God nature, but when I see His hand reaching down into our lives, touching, hallowing the events of each day, I nearly weep with the wonder of it.

Like Mary, crying in the garden outside the empty tomb, I have at times been grief-stricken, confused, lonely. Jesus Himself draws near, but my eyes, like hers, are blinded by tears and I don't recognize Him. He calls me by name and then I know that He, the risen Christ, is in the garden with me. It is a watered garden.